Pensionize Your Nest Egg

Pensionize Your Nest Egg

How to Use Product Allocation to Create a Guaranteed Income for Life

Moshe A. Milevsky, PH.D.
Alexandra C. Macqueen, CFP

WILEY
John Wiley & Sons Canada, Ltd.

Copyright © 2010 Moshe A. Milevsky, Alexandra C. Macqueen

Pensionize™ and Pensionization™ are trademarks of The QWeMA Group.

All rights reserved. No part of this work covered by the copyright herein may be reproduced or used in any form or by any means—graphic, electronic, or mechanical without the prior written permission of the publisher. Any request for photocopying, recording, taping, or information storage and retrieval systems of any part of this book shall be directed in writing to The Canadian Copyright Licensing Agency (Access Copyright). For an Access Copyright license, visit www.accesscopyright.ca or call toll free 1-800-893-5777.

Care has been taken to trace ownership of copyright material contained in this book. The publisher will gladly receive any information that will enable them to rectify any reference or credit line in subsequent editions.

Library and Archives Canada Cataloguing in Publication Data

Milevsky, Moshe Arye, 1967–
Pensionize your nest egg : how to use product allocation to create a guaranteed income for life / Moshe Milevsky, Alexandra Macqueen.

ISBN 978-0-470-68099-5

1. Pensions. 2. Asset allocation. 3. Finance, Personal. I. Macqueen, Alexandra Carol, 1967- II. Title.

HG179.M5183 2010 332.024'014 C2010-901892-3

Production Credits
Cover design: Pat Loi
Interior design: Pat Loi
Typesetter: Thomson Digital
Printer: Solisco Tri-Graphic
Cover image credit: iStockphoto

Editorial Credits
Executive Editor: Karen Milner
Production Editor: Pauline Ricablanca

John Wiley & Sons Canada, Ltd.
6045 Freemont Blvd.
Mississauga, Ontario
L5R 4J3

Printed in Canada

1 2 3 4 5 STG 14 13 12 11 10

Table of Contents

Preface xi

Introduction: Why Retirement Income Is Better than Retirement Savings 1

PART I: WHY YOU NEED TO BUILD YOUR OWN PENSION PLAN: THE MOST PREDICTABLE CRISIS IN HISTORY 5

Chapter 1: The Real Pension Crisis 7

Up a Creek without a Pension Paddle 8

Mixing Defined Benefit Apples and Defined Contribution Oranges 9

It Takes Two to Tango: A Basic Lesson about the Nature of True Pensions 14

Guarantee versus Ruin 15

When Is a Pension Not a Pension? 16

There Ain't No Such Thing . . . as a Free Pension 17

The First True Pensions 19

Chapter 2: Planning for Longevity: Risks While Waiting for Your Return 21

The Grim Reaper's Coin Toss 25

Introducing Longevity Risk 25

Predicting Future Longevity 27

How Should You Insure Against Longevity Risk? 29

Will You Get Heads . . . or Tails? 30

Chapter 3: How the Sequence of Returns Can Ruin Your Retirement 33

How Long will the Money Last? 36

Clockwise Investment Returns 40

Counter-Clockwise Returns 42

Triangles, Bulls, and Bears: The Retirement Income Circus 44

Can Buckets Bail Out a Poor Sequence of Returns? 45

Would Saving More Save Your Retirement? 46

Chapter 4: Inflation: The Great Money Illusion 49

What Does This Mean for Retirees? 52

The CPI-ME and the CPI-YOU 54

Does the CPI Measure YOUR Spending? 55

A Reality Check for Your Retirement Spending? 56

What Did We Learn So Far? 57

PART II: DEVELOPING A SUSTAINABLE RETIREMENT SOLUTION: THE MODERN APPROACH THAT IS HUNDREDS OF YEARS OLD 59

Chapter 5: Beyond Asset Allocation: Introducing the New Science of Product Allocation 61

Product Allocation: New Baskets for Your Nest Egg 61

Three Product Silos 62

The Spectrum of Retirement Income Silos 64

How Do the Silos Stack Up? 65

Chapter 6: An Introduction to Life Annuities 67

Pension Contributions as Insurance Premiums 68

Buying a Personal Pension 69

Converting Your Nest Egg to Retirement Income 71

When Should You Buy an Annuity? 72

Annuities versus GICs 75

Is the Annuity Gamble Worth It? 76

Great-Grandma's Gamble 77

The Power of Mortality Credits 79

What about 50-Year-Olds? Should They Buy Personal Pensions? 80

What about Interest Rates? 82

How Can I Use Annuities to Protect against Inflation? 83

Unique and Peculiar Insurance 84

Chapter 7: A Review of Traditional Investment Accounts 87

Asset Allocation in Your SWP 89

What Should You Put in the SWP? 90

Chapter 8: Introducing the Third Silo—Guaranteed Lifetime Withdrawal Benefit Products 93

Guarantees and Growth: How GLWBs Work 94

GLWBs: Issuers, Features, and Benefits 97

Chapter 9: Your Retirement Sustainability: Fundamental Concepts in Retirement Income Planning 101

Which Glasses Will You Wear? 103

How Many Eggs Can You Withdraw from Your Nest? 104

What Should You Protect Against: Floods or Meteorites? 107

Do You Feel Lucky? Pensions, Survival Probabilities, and Spending in Retirement 108

Pensions Change the Game 108

How Does Pensionization Impact Your Retirement Sustainability Quotient? 110

Pension Annuities: Step-by-Step Math 116

The True Gift of Pensionization 117

Chapter 10: The Most Difficult Question You Will Ever Have to Answer (About Your Retirement) 119

Retirement Sustainability or Financial Legacy? 121

Pricing Your Inheritance 122

Finding Your Spot on the Frontier 124

Chapter 11: Divvying Up Your Nest Egg 127

What Is the Cost to Pensionize? 130

When Should You Pensionize? 132

Summary of Part II 133

PART III: THE SEVEN STEPS TO PENSIONIZE YOUR NEST EGG 135

Chapter 12: Step 1: Identify Your Desired Retirement Income 137

Step 1 - Identify Your Desired Retirement Income 137

Estimating Your Desired Income from the Top Down 141

Estimating Your Desired Income from the Ground Up 141

Recap of Step 1 143

Chapter 13: Step 2: Estimate Your Existing Pensionized Income 145

Canada's Public Pensions 146

Old Age Security 147

The Guaranteed Income Supplement 147

The Quebec and Canada Pension Plans 148

How Much Will You Receive? 149

Benefits from a Defined Benefit Pension Plan 150

What If I'm Worried about the Future of My DB Pension Plan? 152

Timing the Retirement Decision 152

Completing Step 2 153

Recap of Step 2 153

Chapter 14: Step 3: Determine Your Pension Income Gap 155

Your Average Tax Rate 156

Your Pension Income Gap 157

Adjusting for Inflation 159

Recap of Step 3 160

Chapter 15: Step 4: Calculate Your Retirement Sustainability Quotient 163

What Kind of Eggs Do You Have in Your Nest? 163

Filling the Gap 164

Recap of Step 4 168

Chapter 16: Step 5: Assess Your Plan: Is It Sustainable? 169

Recap of Step 5 171

Chapter 17: Step 6: Calculate Your Financial Legacy Value 173

Recap of Step 6 174

Chapter 18: Step 7: Use Product Allocation to Pensionize the Right Fraction of Your Nest Egg 175

Case Study: Jack and Jill Go Up the Hill (to Fetch a Retirement Income Plan) 176

Step 1: Identify Your Desired Retirement Income 177

Step 2: Estimate Your Existing Pensionized Income 178

Step 3: Determine Your Pension Income Gap 178

Step 4: Calculate Your Retirement Sustainability Quotient 179

Step 5: Assess Your Plan: Is It Sustainable? 180

Plan A: Spend Less 181

Plan B: Pensionize a Fraction of Your Nest Egg by Buying an Annuity 181

Step 6: Calculate Your Financial Legacy Value 182

Step 7: Use Product Allocation to Pensionize Your Nest Egg 183

Summary of Part III 184

Final Thoughts 185

Notes 189

Bibliography 193

Acknowledgements 195

About the Authors 197

Index 199

Preface

We're going to ask you to do a lot of speculating, imagining, forecasting, and projecting in this book—and we're going to start now. We're going to open this book with a fable about a hero on a daring quest.

Let's imagine that hero is you. Your quest is to survive a perilous journey while amassing enough gold pieces to sustain you for the rest of your life, once you've reached the journey's end.

So far, you've travelled many miles over treacherous ground, following the path through unexpected twists and turns. And you've been gathering gold pieces along the way, carefully storing them in what you hope are safe havens that you can access once your journey is over.

The good news is that the end of your journey is in sight.

The bad news is that the danger is not over.

Three new risks have emerged from the shadows, standing between you and the caves where you've stored your gold. Let's get a closer look at them: there's the *Dragon of Decaying Dollars*—will it cause your gold to lose its value over time? What about the dreaded

Serpent of the Sequence of Returns—will it unexpectedly make off with half of your fortune? And finally, does the *Spectre of Longevity Risk* loom over you, rendering you paralyzed with worry about running out of gold while you are still alive?

This book is all about getting you past those mythical beasts—and the very real risks they represent—to your ultimate goal: your safe and happy retirement, free from worry about having enough gold to last for the rest of your days.

In this book, we're going to equip you with all kinds of tools, from special glasses to crafty calculators and more, and these will all help you along the way. But to get you to your goal, *we're going to give you the most powerful shield we know*—one that can vanquish all the beasts we've just described while protecting your gold for as long as you live. That shield is *pensionization*.

What is "pensionization?" It is the process of taking a fraction of your nest egg (your hoard of stored gold) and turning it into a guaranteed income that lasts for your lifetime. Pensionizing your nest egg enables you to get where you need to go. It will ensure you have enough income (enough gold pieces) for as long as you need it.

The truth is: your nest egg is probably more fragile than you think, and the strategies you've used to protect yourself up until now won't be sufficient as you move into and through retirement.

In the coming pages, we will examine the new risks you and your nest egg face in retirement, and we'll lay the groundwork for you to safeguard yourself and your financial fortunes.

How to Use This Book

So, is this book for you? Well, it isn't a forum to complain about the state of public policy for Canadians entering retirement. It isn't a platform to agitate for particular changes to Canadian retirement income programs. Nor is it a budgeting book providing tips and tricks about how to save more and spend less. It isn't a retirement planning book with quizzes about your psychological readiness to leave the world of work, or a financial planning book with tables that help you calculate the required withdrawals from your retirement savings accounts over time.

Instead, this is a book designed for all the pensionless Canadians who want, need, and demand a plan to create pension-like income that will sustain them for the rest of their lives. *It is your personal toolkit to pensionize your nest egg.*

Sound good? If so, here's how to use the rest of this book:

- Part I focuses on why you need to build your own pension plan. It includes an overview of the real pension crisis in Canada and the challenges you will face as you ready yourself for the retirement stage of life. You'll learn why asset allocation and other time-honoured rules for building savings on the way to this milestone all fall short when it comes time to convert your savings into a stream of income for the rest of your life. Read this part to see exactly what new risks you need to protect yourself against as you reach retirement, and why.
- Part II introduces the modern solution to securing retirement income (actually, the solution is hundreds of years old). Read this part to understand how product allocation differs from asset allocation, to explore the theoretical arguments for creating a personal pension in retirement, and to get an up-to-date overview of the financial products that are available to help you to pensionize your nest egg.
- Part III shows you the step-by-step process you need to follow to convert your nest egg into a guaranteed stream of income for the rest of your life. Complete with calculators, this chapter gives you the tools you need to create your own personal

pensionized income. Read this part to learn how to design a plan that works for you and your life.

One more note before we get started: when reading this book, you will encounter two authors from completely different backgrounds. One is a professor (in the business, finance, and math fields), and one is a practising financial planner. Occasionally you might read something and think, "What the heck was that about?" Those are probably the parts where the math prof got the upper hand. Don't worry; we will always bring you back to reality (or at least one of us will!). This book is designed to be read and understood by ordinary Canadians, whether you are working through it on your own or talking the ideas through with your financial advisor.

Are you ready? Let's begin.

Introduction

Why Retirement Income Is Better Than Retirement Savings

It is early September in the year 2040, and Gertrude has just turned 85 years old. She is in relatively good health and is enjoying this quiet, uncomplicated stage of her life. She has time for her hobbies, which include membership in her local gardening society and a regular bridge night with friends, and time for her family, who visit most holidays and indulge her on birthdays. Her everyday companions include her small dog, Perky, and the young dog walker she has hired to provide the daily activity Perky needs to keep fit. (Running around the park is a little beyond Gertrude these days.)

Gertrude's income (all in 2010 dollars) consists of about $10,000 per year in Canada Pension Plan, some Old Age Security, about $7,000 in dividends and an additional $40,000 from an indexed life annuity she purchased from an insurance company many years ago. While she doesn't have much in the way of investments, she does have a financial advisor to manage her small stock and bond portfolio. Mainly they talk about how much Gertrude wants to donate to charity each year. In fact, the only money question Gertrude really has to deal with is how to spend the annual income of $50,000 that she receives from her pension and life annuities.

Given her family history, Gertrude worries about Alzheimer's, and she does her best to keep herself mentally and physically active with crossword puzzles and trips to the local pool. She has a social network of friends, and the topic of money is rarely discussed. Certainly Gertrude never brings it up—she decided long ago that she didn't want to spend the rest of her life worrying about these things. That's why she chose, as she was preparing for retirement, to pensionize her retirement savings nest egg by converting some of her savings into a stream of income she couldn't outlive.

Contrast this tranquil picture with another possible future for Gertrude: Gertrude has recently celebrated her 85th birthday. While she is happy to have reached this age, her life is not worry free—she feels stressed and uncertain about the daily financial decisions she needs to make. Even a seemingly simple choice like whether or not to go ahead with the surgery her beloved Chihuahua requires is not straightforward, because Gertrude doesn't know for sure whether the cost of her pet's care will impact her own living expenses.

She does her best to follow the financial papers and the stock markets so she can figure out how much she can withdraw from her portfolio every month, but in the back of her mind she has a rising fear that she's missing important details and making bad decisions. She is also concerned about the cost of her Alzheimer's medication and worries that affordable alternatives may never become available in her lifetime.

Every day Gertrude tells herself that she will make a better attempt to read the information that her financial advisor sent her about a new product that he feels is right for her. But she's been making this promise for weeks now, and the package is still sitting unopened on her kitchen table.

It is the year 2040 and the mutual funds that she was quite comfortable with back when they existed have been replaced by ZQBs, which are the great-grandkids of the ETFs that were popular in the early part of the 21st century. Gertrude's financial advisor—her fourth in the last three decades (the first two died of heart attacks and the third retired)—mentioned to her the last time they met that she might have to reduce her spending from the portfolio because of the great timber market crash of 2037, which caused ZQB yields to contango into backwardation. (Or was it the other way around? She can't quite remember.)

Gertrude's husband, Harry, who passed away a few years ago, always used to handle money issues for both of them. Harry left quite a bit of money to Gertrude, but no instruction manual. Her advisor said she has to make her own decisions, but Gertrude hates making these increasingly-complicated financial decisions. Her friends don't seem interested in talking about money, so she is relying more and more on her financial advisor for his advice. But she only sees or talks to him every few months, and he's not available in the late-night moments when she is most worried about keeping everything together.

Gertrude would love to spend more time doing the things she enjoys—like keeping up with her favourite 3-D TV shows each week and maintaining correspondence with her far-flung extended family—but she doesn't feel able to relax enough to truly enjoy life. Should she go ahead with surgery for her dog, or not? How much can she take out of her portfolio this year, and next year, and the year after that? Should she buy this newfangled financial product or stick with what she already has? Will she ever be able to ignore the financial news, or will she need to open envelopes full of scary and confusing information for the rest of her life?

Parallel Gertrudes: which one is better off? We believe your answer is the same as ours: Gertrude #1 wins. In fact, extensive studies by psychologists have shown that Gertrude #1 is happier than Gertrude #2.

This book is all about making sure *your* Gertrude—that is, your future self—has plenty of *income*, as opposed to enough *money*. So how did Gertrude #1 come out ahead? Easy: she pensionized her nest egg. Thirty years ago she made some smart decisions that converted a fraction of her nest egg into income she can't outlive. As a result, she not only has all the income she needs, she also has a worry-free life. In contrast, aiming to have "enough money" gives you the problems of Gertrude #2.

Not sure about the difference? Read on to learn everything you need to know about creating your own guaranteed income for life.

PART ONE

Why You Need to Build Your Own Pension Plan:

The Most Predictable Crisis in History

1

The Real Pension Crisis

Ottawa Citizen, October 31, 2009 – A lifetime of service, a future of uncertainty: " 'After all our years of service; after everything we've done, this is so unfair,' says a tearful pensioner contending with the loss of a significant portion of his pension from Nortel Networks, a result of the company's filing for bankruptcy protection . . ."

Saskatoon Star Phoenix, March 9, 2010 – Seniors may delay retiring: "Saskatchewan seniors may start delaying retirement in order to safeguard their pension payouts. 'Just because you're in a pension plan doesn't mean you're going to be well-off when you retire,' says an expert on the subject . . ."

Globe and Mail, February 24, 2009 – Ottawa won't aid GM pension plan: "Ottawa says Ontario will have to 'go it alone' if the province wants to help General Motors of Canada Ltd. with the multibillion-dollar shortage in its pension funds . . ."

> *National Post, March 7, 2010 – Surviving the pension tsunami:* "The pension crisis has landed full square in the public consciousness . . . Unfortunately, it is a massive, complex problem that will test the willpower and ingenuity of people and institutions at all levels . . ."
>
> *National Post, June 4, 2008 – Supplementary CPP solution:* "Claude Lamoureux, former CEO, Ontario Teachers' Pension Plan: 'Most industry observers would be hard-pressed to remember the last time a single-employer defined benefit pension plan started up . . . If the trend continues, the only Canadians covered by defined benefit plans will be government employees and Members of Parliament . . .'"

Chances are, if you picked up a Canadian newspaper over the last few months, or even years, you saw many alarming articles reporting on the state of Canada's retirement income system and the place of pensions within it—and lots of agreement about the need for changes. Right now, there's an active debate about the future of pensions in Canada. We are awash in expert commissions, opinions from public-policy think tanks, and calls for reform from ordinary Canadians. But what's the crisis? Why the need for reform? What reform is needed? And what difference does any of this make for you?

Up a Creek without a Pension Paddle

The recent, and very public, debate about the safety of retirement income in Canada is replete with alarming statistics. In particular, reports quoted by all sides in the discussion suggest that only about one-third of Canadians currently belong to a formal, or registered, pension plan. What does belonging to a pension plan mean? Well, the common understanding is that if you participate in a pension plan, when you retire, your work paycheque will seamlessly convert to a retirement paycheque for life.

The unspoken implication, of course, is that the two-thirds of Canadians without formal pensions are up a creek. And in contrast to the lucky third who are pension participants, the majority will be living on cat food in retirement, counting every penny as the days go by, and constantly fretting about outliving their savings (or if they aren't worried, they should be!).

At first glance, the available data seems to support this rather bleak picture. According to Statistics Canada, 32 percent of the Canadian labour force participated in a registered pension plan (RPP) in 2008. So yes, it is clear that the majority of working Canadians—about 68 percent of the workforce—are currently pensionless. Ergo, it is no surprise that the public policy *question du jour* is what to do about those people who aren't fortunate enough, or savvy enough, to participate in a registered pension plan. Surely, conventional wisdom suggests, these are the Canadians most at risk of inadequate retirement savings.

Proposals abound, and much ink has been spilled. Here are some of the issues being debated: do we increase CPP from its current maximum benefit of about $11,200 per year? Do we allow for greater tax-sheltered savings? Do we mandate universal pensions for all employees? The assumption underlying all of these discussions is that the population about whom we should be most concerned is the 68 percent of Canadians who do not belong to a registered pension plan.

Mixing Defined Benefit Apples and Defined Contribution Oranges

But allow us to be contrarians for a moment. We are actually quite concerned not just for the majority with no pension plan, but also for a large fraction of the so-called lucky third—those who *think* they will retire to a guaranteed pension income, when in fact they have nothing of the sort.

To understand this concern, we need to examine what we mean when we talk about pensions. If you are among the people contemplating retirement in the next decade, cast your memory back to what the world of work was like when you first joined it. Twenty-five years ago, the vast majority of the largest employers in North America offered what are known as defined benefit (DB) pensions to their employees. This form of pension **promises a lifetime of income** to each retiree when he or she stops working, with the potential for a survivor pension for your spouse after you die, too. Note our emphasis on "promise" and "lifetime of income"—these are key distinctions in the world of pensions. If you started work for a large company 25 years ago, chances are pretty good that you have a DB pension plan.

But over the last few decades, the proportion of companies offering DB pensions to new employees has steadily dropped. Today, if you work in the public sector, chances are you (still) have a DB pension plan. But if you work in the private sector, your chances aren't so good—if you have a pension plan, it is likely a defined contribution (DC) plan, also known as a money purchase plan. Now, DC pensions are still considered registered pension plans for Statistics Canada purposes, so people who participate in DC plans are included in the lucky third of Canadians who belong to a registered pension plan.

However, DC pensions, despite their name, *are essentially nothing more than tax-sheltered investment plans and offer no promises of lifetime income*. Here's the difference between the two kinds of pension plans: in a defined contribution plan, the amounts *contributed to* the plan are known. In a defined benefit plan, the amounts *paid out* of the plan (the benefits) are known and guaranteed. In a DB plan, certainty comes after retirement. In a DC plan, the only certainty is before retirement.

Exhibit 1.1: Defined Benefit versus Defined Contribution Pension Plans

Defined Benefit	Defined Contribution
Income is determined by a formula based on earnings history and years of service.	Income is determined by the amount the employee contributed, the amount the employer contributes and market performance.
Example: the payout during retirement equals 2 percent X years of service X final salary.	Example: the employee contributes 5 percent of salary and the employer contributes 10 percent.
The employer guarantees a certain benefit level at retirement.	No guaranteed benefit level at retirement.
The employer absorbs all the risk.	The employee absorbs all the risk.
The employer is responsible for paying the pension benefits.	The employer's liability ends after the money is contributed.

In defined contribution pension plans, funds flow into the pension plan from the employer, the employee, or both, are invested in the volatile stock and bond markets, and the gains are tax-deferred until the income is received—*but nowhere is there any mention of a guarantee*. There's no promise of lifetime income. Instead, your retirement future is subject to the random ups and downs of the stock and bond markets. (And in Chapter 3, you'll learn exactly how risky it is to leave the security of your retirement income to the whims of the markets.)

So, given this insight into the differing kinds of pensions available today, let's look again at how many Canadians have a guaranteed income in retirement—a DB pension plan. Exhibit 1.2 provides an overview.

From the pension triangle below, you can see that about 93 percent of the Canadian labour force are considered employed—they are

Exhibit 1.2: Who Is a Member of a Workplace Pension Plan in Canada?

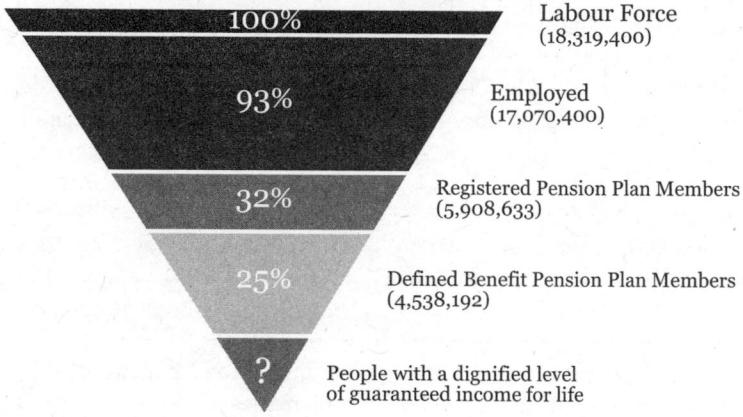

Source: Statistics Canada. Table 282-0089, Table 280-0008 & Table 280-0017 (2008 data).

actively working, not looking for work, on maternity or education leave, or on long-term disability.

The next slice of our triangle shows the number of people who participated in a registered pension plan at their workplace. This slice includes everyone who participated in any kind of pension plan: defined benefit, defined contribution, and other (including what are called hybrid and flex plans, which form a small proportion of the total).

The next slice down identifies the number of people with defined benefit plans, which we have already compared to defined contribution plans.

Finally, the tip of our triangle is reserved for people who have defined benefit plans that will guarantee them a dignified standard of living for the rest of their lives—we don't know the size of this group, but we do know that it is smaller than the number of people with DB plans. As we saw at the outset of this chapter, even DB plans can be withdrawn, collapsed, or redefined without the consent of their members. Ask yourself: which group are you in? Unless you're in the tip of the triangle, this book is for you.

Looking again at our triangle, you can see that some 25 percent of all members of the Canadian labour force participate in a defined benefit pension plan. But let's look more closely at the breakdown in the *type of employment* held by pension plan members.

Exhibit 1.3 shows that if you work in the public sector in Canada, you have a very good chance of participating in a DB pension: 77 percent of public sector workers participated in a DB pension plan in 2008. In contrast, only 17 percent of private sector workers belonged to a DB pension plan.

Exhibit 1.3: Who Is a Member of a DB Pension Plan? Private and Public Sector Workers, 2008

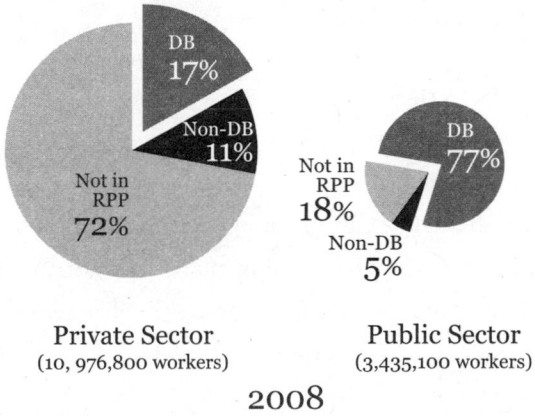

Source: Statistics Canada. Table 280-0008 & Table 282-0089.

What Exhibit 1.3 shows is that if you're not a public servant, the odds are very good that you will not have a genuine pension in retirement. Now, public sector workers may say, "We paid for our pension coverage!"—but the reality is, as a taxpayer, *so did you*; except you won't see any benefit from your contributions. In addition, DB pensions in the public sector are the *only* pensions that come with a government guarantee. These days it seems as though private sector workers are increasingly unlikely to ever get access to the kind of secure lifetime income that their public sector counterparts can count on as a matter of course.

Exhibit 1.4: Percent of Labour Force Who Are Members of a Registered Pension Plan

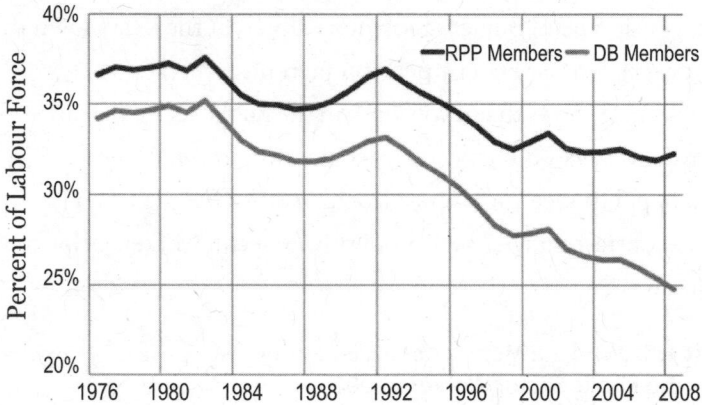

Source: Statistics Canada. Table 280-0008 & Table 282-0089.

Finally, Exhibit 1.4 shows the decline in overall pension coverage, and in DB pension coverage in particular, in the Canadian labour force over the last three decades.

So far, we've shown the decline in pension coverage in Canada as a whole, and in private sector DB pension plans in particular. The main points we want to leave you with so far are the differences between DB and DC plans and the decline in DB plans.

It Takes Two to Tango: A Basic Lesson about the Nature of True Pensions

The current public discussion of the pension crisis in Canada glosses over the vital distinction between DB and DC pensions. Today the term "pension" is used to describe both DB and DC pension plans, with the result that many people who think they have a pension are really members of a collective saving and investment plan or a capital accumulation plan, such as a group Registered Retirement Savings Plan (RRSP), a defined contribution pension plan, or a profit-sharing plan.

So, let's be perfectly clear about what we mean when we talk about pensions in this book. A pension is *not* a synonym for a large sum of money, diversified asset allocation, or a retirement residence in Florida. In our view, even a seven-figure RRSP or DC pension plan balance is not a pension.

Instead, a pension involves a binding contract. A pension includes a guarantee. A pension is a pledge that you—the retiree—will receive a real, predictable, and reliable income stream for the rest of your natural life. A pension is more than an asset class; it is a *product* class. (We'll provide lots more information on asset allocation versus product allocation in Part II. And while the phrase "product allocation" may be new to you now, by the end of this book you'll be an expert in it.)

A true pension also involves more than just you. A true pension tango requires two parties: you, the prospective retiree, and your dance partner, the entity standing behind the promise. The counterparty to the pension promise can be an insurance company, government entity, or corporate pension plan. *But for it to be called a genuine pension there must be somebody guaranteeing something.* No guarantee? No pension.

Guarantee versus Ruin

You may be asking: "Why is a guarantee so important?" The answer is very basic. Our quantitative analysis indicates that a prospective retiree—who could be you—might have 20, 30, or even 40 times their annual income needs in investable wealth (what we would call a Wealth-to-Needs ratio of 20, 30, or 40; and more on this ratio later). These assets could be sitting in the most diversified of mutual funds, investments, RRSPs, or even in a defined contribution pension plan, and yet the retiree still runs the risk that the portfolio will not last as long as he or she does. This is the nature of random and unpredictable human longevity combined with financial volatility. In the language of retirement income planning, retirement income streams without guarantees are subject to a high "lifetime ruin probability"—which happens when you are alive, but your portfolio is dead.

Ironically, both good news (future breakthroughs in medical science) and bad news (unexpected personal inflation or another miserable decade in the stock market) can negatively affect your income prospects in retirement. That is, events on either side of the ledger can wreak havoc on the retirements of even the wealthiest of retirees. (We'll be talking about these kinds of risks in Chapters 2 to 4.)

When Is a Pension Not a Pension?

You may be thinking: "I have a true pension—the DB kind—so I'm free and clear of worry." But are you?

As we've said, if you have a guaranteed lifetime pension, your pension dance partner is supposed to continue to send your monthly cheques, come economic hell or financial high water. Note that this is no trivial promise to make. However, as illustrated in the opening to this chapter, many corporations—from Nortel Networks to United Airlines—have defaulted or are in the process of weaseling out of their simple contracts. Others have given their aging pensioners undesirable financial haircuts by reducing their expected monthly income after the fact. In the last decades, companies have walked away from pension obligations and dumped the problem on governments and the public. Retiring employees, who expected a seamless transition from work paycheque to retirement paycheque, are instead spending their (unpaid!) time battling with former employers about the status of their pension claims. Their promised pensions failed to materialize—their pension partners walked off the dance floor.

Today, a true pension is as rare as it is expensive. We think even the promise of a gold-plated corporate defined benefit pension paying

100 percent of pre-retirement salary, inflation-adjusted for the rest of the retiree's life, is **not** a pension *if the company can renege on the promise by filing for bankruptcy.*

There Ain't No Such Thing . . . as a Free Pension

Now that we've given a sense of the personal value of a true pension, let's talk about the cost.

To get an idea of what a true guaranteed pension will set you back these days, consider the following example. Imagine you're a 62-year-old contemplating early retirement. You ask your favourite A-rated insurance company agent to provide a quote for a personal pension. They offer something in the following price range: for every $10,000 of guaranteed, inflation-adjusted annual income you would like to receive for the rest of your life, you must give us $167,000 up front (in mid-2010, using market rates). Yes, you read that correctly: you need to ante up with nearly *seventeen times* the desired annual income. So let's do the math. If you want $60,000 of inflation-protected annual income for the rest of your life, that'll cost you about a cool million. No, this is no Madoff-like scheme to make off with your RRSP—this is the fair price in the open market for an indexed life annuity, which is the closest thing to a defined benefit pension that exists in the retail market. If this type of retirement income seems too expensive, the market price is telling you something about what true pensions are actually worth. (In later chapters, we'll talk in more detail about the costs of your own, self-purchased pension, including how external variables, such as the inflation rate, affect the amount you can expect to receive.)

Now, you might decide, "Heck, I have $1,000,000 in my RRSP and I can invest it myself to create my own $60,000 pension." Well, here is our warning to you: *there is no risk-free lunch.* There is a very good reason the insurance company charges you what seems to be so much. First, interest rates are abnormally low right now relative to historical rates, which increases the cost of any guarantee. Secondly, and more importantly, by offering you a lifetime income stream, *they* are taking the risk that you'll outlive your savings off your personal balance sheet—and placing it on their corporate balance sheet. Generating $60,000 per year might not seem like much if you have a million to spare, but if you have that viewpoint, you are probably not seeing the whole picture, and it's time to nudge you back to reality. Pensions are expensive because they are valuable, even if you don't think so.

In fact, according to something called the "life-cycle model of consumption"—which is a marvellous tool used by economists to measure consumer demand for consumption, savings, and investment from cradle to grave—the true value of a true pension is astonishingly high. To understand how the life-cycle model operates, think of it as a bathroom scale. You can use the scale to measure the weight of any item, even if you can't weigh it directly. For example, if you stand on the bathroom scale fully clothed and then do the same totally naked, you can calculate the weight of your clothes even if you never put them directly on the scale.

The model can be used in this way to measure the "utility value," or perceived usefulness, of a pension. To make a long and complex mathematical story short, the utility value of a pension can be worth up to half of your typical net worth. One implication of this finding is that a rational retiree (risk-averse, healthy, and pensionless) would rather have $500,000 worth of pension than $1,000,000 worth of cash, given the choice of only one. Yes, you read that one correctly as well. The message from this model is that most Canadians would be willing to pay—keeping in mind that willingness to pay is a fundamental concept in economics—a large premium to exchange their cash for pensions. (We'll delve further into the life-cycle model and how it applies to the world of pensions in Chapter 9.)

The First True Pensions

Back in 1881, the German Chancellor, Otto von Bismarck, introduced the first old age pension and basically invented pensions as we know them today. These old age pensions were to be paid by the state to all its elderly citizens. Notice that he didn't introduce a tax-sheltered savings plan or create some group defined contribution plan. Bismarck's intentions, instead, were to collectively force children to care for their parents in a dignified manner during their golden years, akin to how families cared for their elderly prior to the industrial revolution. The risk was shifted from the old retiree to the young worker and was backed by a solid counterparty, the government. Ergo, *this was a pension.*

Before we go any further, it's worth noting that you might already have access to a minimal amount of true pension income at retirement. Old Age Security, the Guaranteed Income Supplement (GIS), and the Canada and Quebec pension plans have built-in guarantees and risk shifting, which are the hallmarks of true pensions. Despite the rather modest payments they provide, they are guaranteed, in real terms, for your lifetime. Q/CPP, OAS, and the GIS are pensions in the true insurance, financial, and economic senses of the word. There is counterparty to the contract, the Government of Canada, standing behind the guarantee.

Okay. So what does all of this mean for you? Here's the main message of this chapter: while ordinary Canadians and our politicians continue to debate the merits of private versus public provision of pensions, let's make sure you understand exactly what a pension really is. No more mixing up DB and DC pensions, and no more assuming DC pensioners are in the same boat as their DB counterparts. If you have a DC pension, you don't have the kind of smooth ride ahead that your DB counterparts can expect in retirement—unless you pensionize (part of) your nest egg. Finally, if you think your retirement income is safe because you have a job with a pension plan, you may want to check not only the type of plan you are in and what your income replacement rate will be in retirement (60 percent of your working income? 70 percent? 80 percent?), but also consider whether you're comfortable sharing the risk for your income stream in retirement with your employer over the 25, 30, or even 40 years of your retirement.

With all that said, the rest of this book is built on three core beliefs:

1. **The decline in pensions is real.** And not only is it real: it's likely to speed up. No new pensions are coming, existing pensions are disappearing, and it's time for you to recognize and act from this new reality. You need to do something now to prepare for the years ahead—and that is to take responsibility for your own retirement income planning instead of waiting for politicians to bring back 1950s-style pensions.
2. **True pensions provide the guarantees and certainty Canadians require.** A true pension starts at some advanced age and guarantees predictable income that matches the increasing cost of living for retirees. These kinds of pensions are rare and expensive. Don't underestimate the value of true pensions and the protection they provide—especially if you do not belong to a DB pension plan (and even if you haven't got a clue how pension plans work). Like the life-cycle model shows, a true pension is worth its weight in gold.
3. Finally, much ink has been spilled about ways to fix the problems in Canada's current retirement income landscape—but you don't have to wait for change or leave it in anyone else's hands. **This book provides you with all the essential tools you need to create your own pension plan for a secure retirement.**

2

Planning for Longevity: Risks While Waiting for Your Return

Retirement planning, as practised by most financial advisors and planners in Canada, usually begins with a discussion of your money, investments, RRSPs, and RRIFs. Now, while the question of how much to save for retirement is very important, we believe the process of retirement *income* planning should actually begin at the very end—the end of life, that is.

Accordingly, the best place to start planning for retirement income is the obituary section of the *Globe & Mail*, *Toronto Star*, or *National Post*. Yes, this may sound like a gloomy way to begin thinking about what's supposed to be the most rewarding period of your life, but hold on for a few minutes—you'll see the point soon.

So, gather these one or two pages from the newspaper—the section does seem to grow over time, doesn't it?—and collect them for a few days, or even a few weeks. Sit yourself down with a blank piece of paper, a cup of coffee, and a pen. Now, look over each one of the lives chronicled in the obituaries and note the exact age at which these people died. Okay, spend some time reading about their lives and loved ones, but make sure to circle each age of death. Notice how some people lived to a glorious old age of 95, or perhaps even 100, while others barely made it to 70. In some very sad cases you will see ages in the 40s and 50s, and perhaps even 20s and 30s, but those are rare. Most people live well into their so-called retirement years. Circle these numbers and keep track of them.

Next, create a table showing the number of years that each one of these people lived beyond the age of 65, which is a proxy for the numbers of years they spent in the retirement stage of life. Don't write down the negative numbers for the unfortunate few who didn't make it to 65; stay focused on the positive. Subtract 65 from the age at death and write down the resulting number on your pad of paper. So, if somebody passed away at 85, write down the number 20 (= 85−65). If they lived to 97, write down the number 32; if they lived to 66, write down the number 1; and if they died on their 65th birthday (now, what are the odds of that?), write down the number 0. Hopefully you get the point and can create a long list of retirement longevity numbers like this: 27, 23, 14, 2, 7 . . . Bingo!

All joking aside, if you collect these numbers for a few days or weeks, your table should look something like Exhibit 2.1 below. This is a larger and more precise collection—notice the decimal points for fractions of years—recently created by a researcher at The QWeMA Group (www.qwema.ca), a company that creates software algorithms and product solutions for retirement income planning. There are 50 numbers in the table, showing 50 people who passed away over a few weeks in late 2009 and early 2010.

Hidden in those numbers were some interesting lives lived: some famous politicians and actors, a well-known writer, and even a few sports legends. We decided not to include the names for the sake of anonymity, but look carefully at the table. Notice how some people spent just a few years in the retirement stage of life, while others

Exhibit 2.1: Read the Obituaries: How Many Years Did They Spend in Retirement?

8.7	32.0	5.0	14.1	41.4
17.9	17.1	22.2	30.6	25.2
31.0	14.8	7.6	19.0	15.8
8.4	11.3	23.4	40.0	16.1
21.3	23.6	24.1	13.3	17.4
15.5	12.0	22.4	7.7	14.9
27.0	21.8	9.3	21.2	14.5
18.8	29.8	10.9	21.0	11.9
8.2	16.1	15.0	27.0	6.9
38.0	11.9	13.3	10.5	15.4

spent decades. You can see that three people lived to at least 100, one (female) made it all the way to 106 (=65 + 41.4). Spend some time to appreciate the variation or dispersion in those numbers, and ponder the question:

> *Do you think they knew how long they would be spending in the retirement phase of life?*

And how long *did* they spend, on average? If you calculate the arithmetic average of years in retirement—that is to say, you add them all up and divide by 50—you will get the number 18.4. Thus, the average amount of time these people spent in the so-called retirement stage of life was approximately 18 years. Yet some people spent almost 40 years in retirement and some barely made it for a few months—the variation is quite large!

Statisticians have a longstanding way of measuring this variation: they call it the "standard deviation," which measures the spread or dispersion of a set of data around the mean (average) value. The standard deviation for our set of numbers is 8.7, or about 9 years. This means that most of the longevity numbers fall between

18.4 years *plus* 8.7 years, which is 27.1 years, and 18.4 years *minus* 8.7 years, which is 9.7 years.

If this is getting more technical than you care for, Exhibit 2.2 gives a graphical representation of Canadian retirement longevity, together with a picture of the standard deviation just computed. It tells you all you need to know about time spent in retirement. You can see that the number of years spent in retirement roughly follows a kind of bell-shaped curve, like so many other things in life. More importantly, as you can see, *the number of years you spend in retirement is random!*

Exhibit 2.2: Remaining Lifetime for a 65-Year-Old Canadian

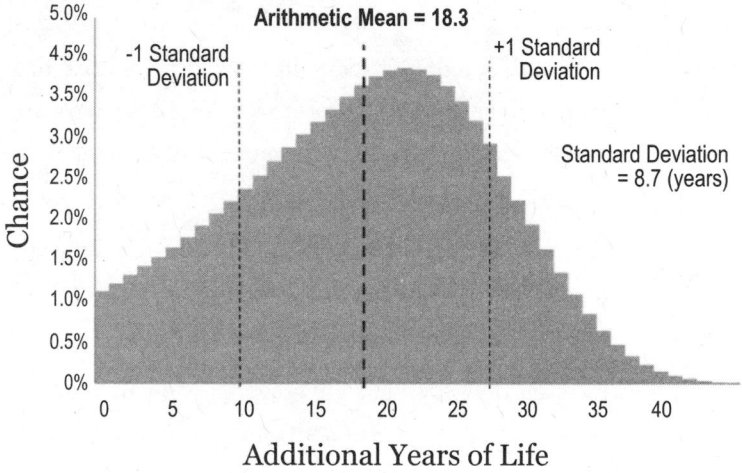

Source: Computations by the QWeMA Group based on Statistics Canada Catalogue No. 84-537-XIE.

Here's the take away from all this discussion of variations and standard deviations: you don't really know how long you might live and thus how much you'll need to save for retirement. You might live as long as 40 years (at the right-hand side of the curve) or, sadly, it might be as short as 2 years (at the left-hand side of the curve). This variability is just as risky as that of the stock market, but stock market risk probably worries you more!

The Grim Reaper's Coin Toss

In fact, one way to think of your chances of differing retirement years is like a Grim Reaper coin toss. If your toss comes out tails, your number will fall to the left of (below) the average, and if it comes out heads, it will fall to the right of (above) the average. We can't overemphasize how random this period can be, and that's just looking at existing data. In the future, medical breakthroughs, scientific achievements, and many other unknown factors can only *increase* this uncertainty.

How so? Just as one example, recent research seems to indicate that people with a heart condition who also have a high intake of omega-3 fatty acids—which are contained in many fish, such as salmon—have relatively longer stretches of DNA, and this length correlates with longevity. So, according to this research, if we can get everyone to eat more fish, then the entire curve in Exhibit 2.2 will shift to the right, and the average amount of time spent by everyone in retirement will increase. Of course, that assumes the mercury in fish won't kill us first—and shift the entire curve to the left. Who knows with these things? So here is the bottom line once again: *your longevity is just as uncertain as the gyrations and fluctuations of stock markets.* Even if you think you can predict your longevity based on your family history, your health status and habits, or your gender—the truth is, you'd be making a very risky bet.

Introducing Longevity Risk

Pension experts—also known as insurance actuaries—call the concept underlying exhibits 2.1 and 2.2 longevity risk. This concept is at the core of many of the products you will read about in the next few chapters of this book. "Longevity risk" describes the risk that results from the fact that the precise length of time you will spend in retirement (and thus how many years of income you need to provide for yourself) is unknown. And here's the kicker—unlike the stock market, where taking on some risk is related to higher expected returns—longevity risk is entirely uncompensated. There's no (financial) payoff from a long life!

Another way to think about or represent longevity risk is by using a "probability distribution." Exhibit 2.3 gives you exactly that. These numbers were collected by researchers at Statistics Canada and are based on millions of obituaries over thousands of days, so this is a lot more scientific than the little experiment you (and we) ran with our coffee and newspapers. These researchers also took population trends into account and made a number of other projections as well. The biostatistics underlying this kind of table are beyond the scope of this book, but the take away is of relevance just the same. Notice that the probability of living to any given age in the next couple of decades after retirement is high.

Exhibit 2.3: Conditional Probability of Survival at Age 65

To Age	Female (%)	Male (%)	At least one member of a couple
70	94.4	90.6	99.5
75	86.0	77.3	96.8
80	73.5	59.4	89.2
85	55.5	38.2	72.5
90	33.2	18.3	45.4
95	14.1	5.5	18.8
100	3.5	0.9	4.4

Source: Computations by the QWeMA Group based on Statistics Canada Catalogue No. 84-537-XIE.

You can see from our table that the probability that a 65-year-old Canadian female will survive to age 95 is 14 percent, while the probability that a 65-year-old male will live to 95 is just 5.5 percent. (Keep in mind that these numbers are for the entire population, not just two people!)

Here is yet another important lesson about longevity (and its risk)—it is measurably higher for females than it is for males. In fact, if you paid attention while reading the obituary section, you would have noticed that although some females passed away at a relatively young age and some males passed away at a relatively old age, on average the retired females lived longer than the retired males. What this means from a practical point of view is that *women must plan for a longer retirement.*

Predicting Future Longevity

Some readers might wonder how (and where) exactly the numbers in all these exhibits come from and whether you can rely on them in making predictions or planning for the future. After all, it's one thing to display the age at which people died in the past, but how can you know the age at which people will die in the future? This question is a good one, but in the absence of any evidence to the contrary, the statisticians are assuming that history will repeat itself. If the obituaries over the last few years result in exhibits similar to 2.1 and 2.2, the assumption is that obituaries in 20, 30, or more years from now—including yours!—will exhibit the same pattern. Sure, there might be some improvements for the average, and you might get lucky, but the variation will always be there.

Take a look at Exhibit 2.3 again. There is a third column that shows the probability that at least one member of a couple will survive over a given period. Notice that the odds of one person in a couple living to a given age are *larger* than the odds of an individual living for the same time period. To compute the probability of at least one member of a couple living to a given age, we calculate the chance of one person living to that age, and then, independently, the odds of the other person living to that age. Then the probability that at least one member of a couple lives to that age is calculated as one minus the probability that they both die before that age.

The implication is that if you are married, the chance that one of you will live to age 95 (or any other age in the spectrum) is greater than your individual chance of living to that age. So if you are married, you need to take this joint probability into account in your planning, rather than relying on your individual probability of survival over time.

Finally, here is yet another important detail from Exhibit 2.3. Notice how the numbers in all three columns start off close to 100 percent and get closer to zero with age. This declining pattern can be plotted in a graph, which is what you see in Exhibit 2.4.

Exhibit 2.4 is often called a *survival probability curve*, and it provides a quick visual illustration of the fact that the odds of living longer decline exponentially with time and age. Very few people

Exhibit 2.4: Longevity Probabilities for Men and Women—Age 65 and Up

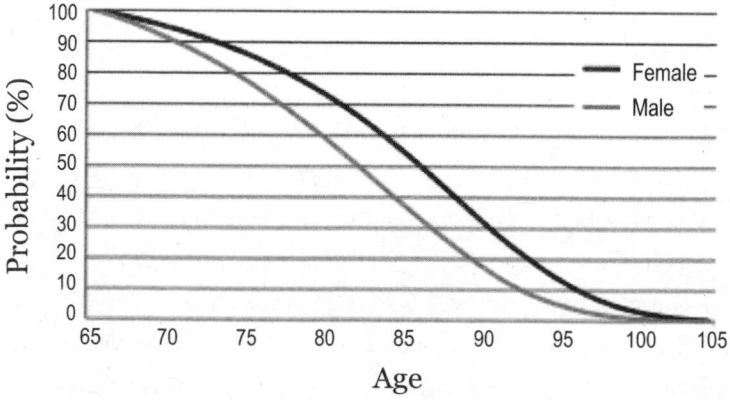

Source: Statistics Canada - Catalogue No. 84-537-XIE.

currently aged 65 will make it to 105 and few of them will die before age 75. The information conveyed in Exhibit 2.4 is exactly the same as the information in Exhibit 2.3.

Remember, if you aren't alive, you are dead—so the two probabilities (the probability of survival and the probability of death) add up to 100 percent. The math can't get any easier than that!

How Should You Insure Against Longevity Risk?

What we saw in the previous section is that the human lifespan is random. This insight makes retirement planning more difficult, because we don't know with certainty—or in advance—when any of us will die and, thus, how long our money needs to last. As we've said, the risk we face of mismatching our finite financial resources to our lifespan is known as longevity risk.

Now that you have a basic understanding of longevity risk—what it is and why it's relevant—you are ready to perform some simple retirement income arithmetic. Later chapters will do the math in greater depth and with more accuracy, but for now we'll keep things simple. Imagine you are approaching your 60s and thinking seriously about retiring in the next few years. How much money do you need in your nest egg to finance your retirement?

Assume for the moment that you want an income or cash flow of exactly $50,000 per year to maintain your desired lifestyle. (This, too, will be addressed more carefully in later chapters to account for federal and provincial income taxes, CPP, inflation, and more. Again, we'll keep it simple for now.)

Continuing with our example, if you end up living in retirement for 40 years, you need approximately $50,000 times 40, which is $2,000,000, in your nest egg (ignoring interest, investment gains, the time value of money, and so on). But if you only end up living five years in retirement—and you saw some of these examples back in

Exhibit 2.1—then you only need $50,000 times 5, which is $250,000, in your RRSP or retirement account. As you can see, the difference between millions and hundreds of thousands—*both legitimate estimates of what you might need*—is enormous. And yet here's the catch: you don't know until after the fact if you need the big number or the small number.

If only you could read your obituary's date before you start retirement, financial life would be so much easier to plan for. (Now there's a thought!)

Will You Get Heads . . . or Tails?

But this uncertainty is precisely why longevity risk is more than just a morbid actuarial curiosity. It has real financial implications. Think about this: you spend your entire working life diligently saving every extra dollar, diversifying, carefully allocating your assets, investing the maximum in your RRSP and Tax Free Savings Account (TFSA), all so you can retire with a million-dollar nest egg. But then, after a few years of retirement living, the bulk of the nest egg goes to somebody else because you got tails on the longevity risk coin toss. Sure, bequeathing all that money to your loved ones might not be such a bad thing—but is that why you were frugal for 30 working years?

Consider the other end of the spectrum: you might have built up a medium-sized nest egg, planning for an average retirement of about 25 years, only to get heads on the longevity coin toss and live 30, 35, or even more years after age 65. This outcome means that you will either have to reduce your standard of living or perhaps even borrow from your kids or against your assets. In either case, this is a very inefficient way to manage this stage of your life; it's like planning for a dinner party without having any idea how many guests will show up.

Get the point? Is this really a risk you want to take? Remember: DB pensions protect against this risk.

Now, one of the main concepts underlying this book is that many Canadians are exposing themselves to longevity risk and probably don't know it yet. We believe that this is a risk that *can* be avoided, or at least managed properly, by pensionizing your nest egg—that is, taking some of your financial assets and converting them to a pension that pays a guaranteed income for the rest of your life. Pensionizing will protect you against the uncertainty about the length of your life and against numerous other risks you might face and may not even know about.

Many Canadians are exposing themselves to longevity risk. We believe this is a risk that can be avoided, or at least managed properly, by pensionizing your nest egg—that is, taking some of your financial assets and converting them to a personal pension, or indexed life annuity, that pays a guaranteed income for the rest of your life.

Curious? Read on.

3

How the Sequence of Returns Can Ruin Your Retirement

We know that in the back of your mind you might be wondering, "But isn't a solid portfolio of stocks and bonds good enough to finance my retirement?" After all, the mutual fund industry has been preaching that, over the long term, there is no better place for your money than its mutual funds. This question brings us to the topics of downside protection and the curse of the sequence of returns. And no, this curse isn't some ancient medieval wizardry.

For many years members of the financial services industry—egged on by the media and even academics (but we're not naming names)—have preached the virtues of stocks, equity, and the buy-and-hold theory of investing. No doubt you have seen mountain-like charts of what a mere $1 invested back in the year 1881 would have grown to by the year 2010. You might have also heard that the compound rate of return (or growth rate) from a diversified portfolio of stocks has been around 7 percent, after inflation, during the last century or so. This is true. We don't dispute any of it. But it also might be completely irrelevant when it comes to retirement income planning, and here is why.

Let's look at what stock markets have actually done for investors. We created returns for three imaginary investors: Sally, Robert, and David. Each of our characters invested $1,000 every month for a total of 15 years, for a total of $180,000 invested. However, they each followed a different investment strategy. Sally put all her funds in one-month Treasury Bills. Robert put all of his funds in the Canadian stock market (proxied by the TSX). David put all of his funds in stock markets too, but he diversified outside of Canada: he put 75 percent of his investments in the Canadian stock market and 25 percent in the U.S. stock market (proxied by the S&P 500).

Consider that saving $1,000 per month for 15 years is a significant effort toward building a retirement nest egg. So how did each of our investors do?

Conventional wisdom suggests that David and Robert will have done better than Sally: many believe that by taking on the additional investment risk of investing in the markets, not guaranteed investments, they will be rewarded with additional returns. But is that true? Is 15 years—an average retirement savings timeframe—a sufficiently long enough time to count on the rewards of buy-and-hold stock market investing?

In Exhibit 3.1, we show some results for 15 years of saving, ending in the years 1998 (for a saver starting in 1983) to (March) 2010 (for a saver starting in 1995).

We've highlighted the highest and lowest ending values for each fictional saver. Based on the conventional wisdom about the rewards of investment risk, diversification, and the buy-and-hold strategy, you'd expect that David would end up on top, followed by Robert, with both trailed by Sally. But by looking at Exhibit 3.1, you can see that the results show a lot of variability. Yes, there are periods when David and Robert are much better off. David has both the highest and the lowest results—his is the strategy with the most variable results.

Exhibit 3.1: 15 Years of Monthly Saving—Does a Buy-and-Hold Strategy Pay Off?

	Fifteen Years of $1,000 of Monthly Saving = $ 180,000 Invested (CAD)		
	Sally	**Robert**	**David**
Nest Egg	**T-Bill**	**TSX**	**75% TSX, 25% S&P500**
Low	$225,029	$230,410	$206,885
High	$303,923	$470,708	$531,187
Range	$78,894	$240,298	$324,302

Source: Computations by the QWeMA Group based on data from Standard and Poor's & Bank of Canada.

Now, we want to make absolutely clear that in no way shape or form are we disparaging the stock market or equities as a means for accumulating wealth. In fact, we are huge fans of share-ownership and have substantial amounts of our financial capital invested in exchange traded funds (ETFs) and mutual funds that hold equities. We are both relatively young with long time horizons and secure jobs (or "bond-like" human capital allocations). Moreover, we are fully cognizant of the risks involved in equity investing and are willing to expose ourselves to these risks. The monies we have set aside are not required or absolutely necessary for our retirement income. But, for those readers counting on this random, unpredictable and extremely volatile pot of money to sustain them through retirement, they must beware of the fact that 15 years isn't enough time to wash-out the risks. This is one of the great lessons from the recent financial crisis.

Exhibit 3.2 was created from the same data, and it shows four arbitrary retirement dates at which either Sally, David, or Robert came

Exhibit 3.2: Three Savings Strategies, Four Arbitrary Retirement Dates: Which One Wins?

	Sally	Robert	David
Retire at the End of . . .	**T-Bill**	**TSX**	**75% TSX, 25% S&P500**
Oct. 2004	$249,061	$300,822	$303,786
Jul. 2008	$237,098	$373,003	$316,745
May 2009	$231,840	$230,410	$206,886
Mar. 2010	$225,030	$272,345	$238,163

Source: Computations by the QWeMA Group based on data from Standard and Poor's & Bank of Canada.

out on top. You can see that each fictional saver "wins" at different times—there is no clear-cut strategy for amassing the most retirement savings.

To make matters worse, in Exhibit 3.1 and 3.2 we assumed relatively modest investment fees of only 2 percent on the stock investments. However, the average fees on equity mutual funds in Canada hover around 2.5 percent—so if David and Robert were investing using equity mutual funds with average fees, their results would be worse. We note, as well, that fewer than 5% of actively managed Canadian equity mutual funds actually beat the index results over the past 5 years and fewer than 10% of U.S. equity mutual funds beat the U.S. index. So, if we'd assumed average (not index) returns for our equity investors, they'd be worse off for this reason, too!

How Long Will the Money Last?

Perhaps you are approaching retirement and you have a lump sum nest egg valued at $500,000, $750,000, or even $1,000,000 or more.

No matter what T-bills and markets have done up until now, you are looking forward, not backward, and you are ready to turn your retirement savings account into income for life. But (despite what you read earlier in the chapter) let's say you are not ready to think about buying a personal pension. Instead, you want to create a retirement income plan using what the financial services industry calls a Systematic Withdrawal Plan, or SWP—which enables you to sell a varying number of investment units to provide a constant monthly income (think dollar-cost averaging in reverse).

WHAT IS A SYSTEMATIC WITHDRAWAL PLAN?

A systematic withdrawal plan (SWP) is a combination of an investment asset allocation portfolio and a plan to withdraw a fixed dollar amount of money from the portfolio over time, without any regard for whether the portfolio and investments are doing well (up) or not (down).

A fundamental characteristic of a SWP is that the assets in this portion of your portfolio offer no guarantees, no downside protection, and no protection from longevity risk.

A SWP can also be thought of like the opposite of a dollar-cost-averaging (DCA) plan in which a fixed amount of money is used to automatically and periodically purchase stocks or mutual fund units regardless of price. The SWP is like a DCA in reverse. Although it isn't a product *per se*, it is meant to achieve the same thing as a pension; that is, provide a monthly stream of income—at least until the account runs out of money.

The first question you may be asking yourself is, "*How long will my money last?*" Let's answer this question using a simple example assuming a retirement savings nest egg of $100,000. (Now, we know this is a small nest egg. We are keeping our example simple, and remember, the example we're about to show works for nest eggs of any size.)

The basic laws of arithmetic tell us with unwavering accuracy exactly how long a nest egg will last when you make fixed withdrawals (that is, if you withdraw the same amount consistently) and generate known returns (that is, if your investment return does not fluctuate).

For example, if your current $100,000 portfolio is subjected to monthly withdrawals of $750 (which is $9,000 annually) and is earning a nominal rate of 7 percent per year (or 0.5833 percent per month), your nest egg will be completely empty during month 259. Start this (doomed) process at age 65 and you will become ruined (that is, run out of money) halfway through age 86. Exhibit 3.3 illustrates the smooth and predictable path your portfolio will take on its way to ruin.

In this scenario, we know the inevitable date upon which you will run out of money with absolute certainty, as the finance textbooks teach us that the present value of $750 for 260 periods under a

Exhibit 3.3: Portfolio Ruin with Constant Withdrawals and Constant Returns

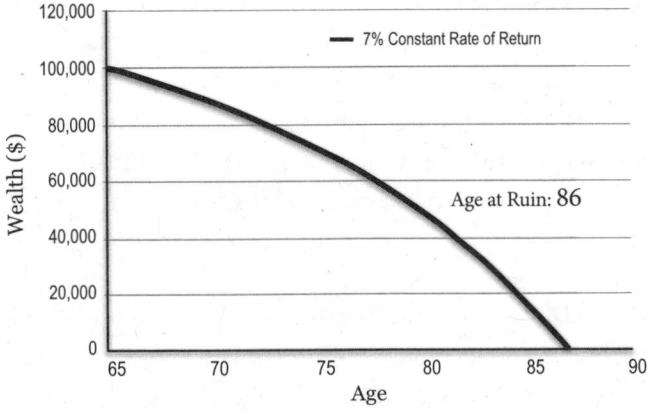

periodic rate of 0.583 percent is exactly $100,000. Ergo, your $100,000 will only last until age 86.5. So, if you plan to live to exactly age 86.5, you should be fine. (By the way, this example holds with a portfolio of $200,000 and withdrawals of $18,000 per year, with a portfolio of $300,000 and withdrawals of $27,000 per year, and so on.)

Of course, if you plan to withdraw a lower $625 per month (which is $7,500 per year), the money runs out by month 466, and the nest egg lasts beyond the age of 100 for the same 65-year-old retiree. (The present value of $625 paid over 465.59 periods under a periodic rate of 0.5833 percent is also $100,000.)

So, if you knew *for sure* when you'd die and you knew *for sure* what your investments would earn over your lifetime, you could design a great retirement income plan.

But what happens if you (the hypothetical 65-year-old retiree) do not earn a constant 7 percent each and every year, but instead earn an *arithmetic average* of 7 percent over your retirement? How long does the money last, how variable is the final outcome, and what does that final outcome depend on?

Remember, investment returns fluctuate in this scenario (and in real life)—and you cannot rely on getting 7 percent every single year, even if you do earn it on average. For example, the Canadian stock market, as proxied by the TSX Composite Index, earned 17.3 percent in the year 2006, 9.8 percent in the year 2007, −33.0 percent in the year 2008, and 35.1 percent in the year 2009. The average of those four years was 7.3 percent—*but that was a far cry from what happened in any given year.*

Now, since there are so many ways to generate an average return of 7 percent, let's give some structure to our problem. Imagine that the annual investment returns are generated in a cyclical and systematic manner. Exhibit 3.4 illustrates how it would work with a simple triangle—each point of the triangle represents a different year and a different investment return.

Exhibit 3.4: Illustrating a 7% Average Return

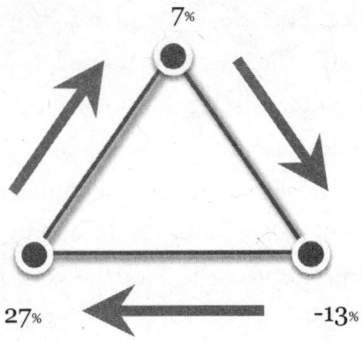

"Clockwise" Return

Clockwise Investment Returns

You can see from our exhibit that during the first year of retirement the portfolio earns 7 percent. In the second year of retirement it earns −13 percent, and in the third year of retirement it earns 27 percent. The arithmetic average of these numbers is exactly 7 percent, and each month we plan on withdrawing the same $750 as in the earlier case. In the fourth year we start the cycle again, and this cyclical process continues in three-year increments until the nest egg is exhausted and the money is gone. So here's the million-dollar question:

> *Do you think you will run out of money earlier or later than in the prior case, where returns were a smooth 7 percent each and every year?*

If you think the answer is *earlier*, you are right. Indeed, since you started retirement on the wrong foot, generating a negative return (−13 percent) *before* the strongly positive return (+27 percent), you will run out of money a full three years earlier, at age 83. The 27 percent return in your third, sixth, and ninth (and so on) years of retirement isn't enough to offset the −13 percent returns in the second, fifth, and eighth (and so on) years of retirement. (This is akin to this year's 20 percent bull market failing to undo the damage of last year's 20 percent bear market.)

Note that the results in the cyclical returns scenario can be computed with just as much accuracy as they can in the constant return scenario, although you can't use a simple formula for the present value in this case. Instead, you must do this manually (what we like to call the "brute force" method).

Here's how to calculate the present value in this case:

- Take out a piece of paper and calculator. Start with $100,000 and force it to earn 0.5833 percent in the first month.
- Then withdraw $750 and have the remaining sum earn 0.5833 percent for the next month.
- Do this for 12 months, and then repeat for 12 months under an investment return of −1.0833 percent per month, which is a nominal −13 percent per year.
- Next, repeat for a further 12 months using an investment return of 2.2500 percent per month, which is a nominal 27 percent per year.

Exhibit 3.5: Portfolio Ruin with a "Clockwise" Sequence of Returns

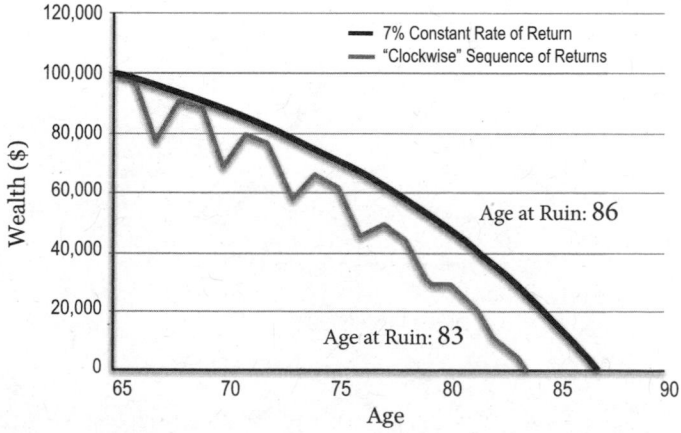

You can see that every 36 months the pattern repeats itself: start with twelve 0.5833 percent numbers, then twelve −1.0833 percent numbers, and finally twelve 2.2500 percent numbers. You should have a very long column of returns that, when charted, mimics the picture in Exhibit 3.5, with the account ultimately reaching zero shortly after your eighty-third birthday. In this case, an average of 7 percent is *worse* than a smooth return of 7 percent every year.

Counter-Clockwise Returns

Now, what happens if you reverse the triangle and instead start in the other direction? In other words, what happens if you earn 7 percent, then 27 percent, and then −13 percent over and over again? Exhibit 3.6 displays the same triangle, but with the arrows going in the other direction.

Remember, the arithmetic average investment return is the same 7 percent regardless what side of the triangle is up when you start retirement earnings and withdrawals. However, this time around the money runs out at age 89.5, as opposed to at ages 83.33 and 86.5 as we saw in Scenarios 1 and 2. So, in this case, getting the highest returns

Exhibit 3.6: Reversing the Sequence of Returns

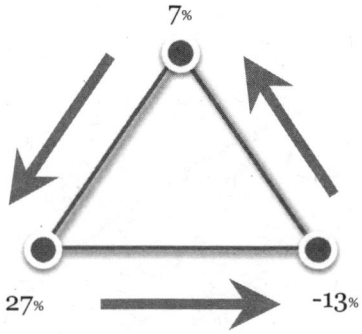

"Counter-Clockwise" Return

Exhibit 3.7: Portfolio Ruin with a "Counter-Clockwise" Sequence of Returns

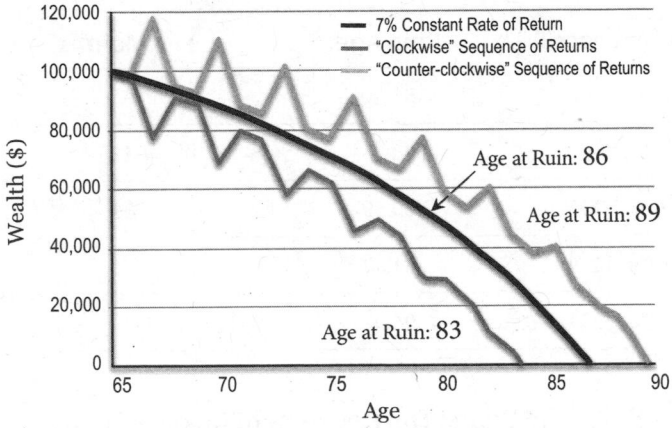

before the negative return is *better* than getting 7 percent every year—it gives you *more* money than earning a constant 7 percent return would. Exhibit 3.7 shows this graphically.

Before we move on, it's worth noting that this variance in outcomes would be even greater if we started with a particularly large number, such as −13 percent or 27 percent, as opposed to the 7 percent return we used as the starting year's return in all cases. For example, if the sequence was −13 percent, 7 percent, and then 27 percent, the age at which you run out of money would be 81—the youngest yet. And if you started with 27 percent, not 7 percent, you'd run out of money at 94.92 years—the highest of all possible scenarios we examined.

Finally, Exhibit 3.8 summarizes the impact of all these various sequences on the "ruin age" (the age at which you run out of money), as well as the variation in months between the given sequence and the baseline case of a constant 7 percent return. You can see that this sequencing gap can get quite large—there is a 14-year gap between the lowest and highest ruin ages.

Exhibit 3.8: What Stop Did You Get on the Retirement Merry-Go-Round? The Impact of the Sequence of Returns on Portfolio Longevity

Return Sequence	Ruin Age	+/– Months
+7%, +7%, +7%...	86.50	–
+7%, **–13%,** +27%...	83.33	–38
+7%, +27%, **–13%**...	89.50	+36
–13%, +7%, +27%...	81.08	–65
+27%, +7%, **–13%**...	94.92	+101

Triangles, Bulls, and Bears: The Retirement Income Circus

To be sure, the market doesn't move in perfect triangles. It is generally believed that stock markets, interest rates, and investment returns move in periodic cycles. These cycles—which also contain substantial "noise," or price and volume fluctuations that are random and meaningless—only become evident with hindsight, and are hence very difficult to predict or measure in advance. Nevertheless, these cycles can have a profound impact on the sustainability of your retirement income.

The bottom line is that if you retire and start to withdraw money from a diversified investment portfolio just as the market moves into a bear cycle, when markets are down, then your portfolio's longevity can be at risk.

IMPACT OF RETIRING IN A BEAR MARKET

If you retire in a bear market, your nest egg will definitely not last as long as it would under an equivalent spending plan that started during a bull cycle. When you are saving money, in the "accumulation phase," a dollar grows to the same value no matter in what order you earn the returns.

This relatively obvious observation is often called the "sequence-of-returns risk." You are most at risk from a negative sequence of returns during the so-called "retirement risk zone"—the years immediately preceding and following retirement, when you have the largest amount of money at stake, the fewest number of years left in the workforce, and thus the smallest capacity to recover from market downturns.

Can Buckets Bail Out a Poor Sequence of Returns?

Now, despite everything we've just said, you may be thinking, "I can protect myself from a poor sequence of returns by putting an amount equivalent to a few years of my income needs into safe investments. Then if the rest of my investments go down, I just won't touch them until the markets recover." This is often called the "bucketing" strategy—where income needs for the first few years of retirement are segregated from the rest of the investment portfolio and placed in safe "buckets." However, although this strategy gives the illusion of safety, in actuality it exposes your nest egg to more risk.

Think about it this way. If you start with an allocation of 50 percent cash and 50 percent equities and plan to draw from the cash bucket to meet your income needs in the first few years of retirement, then as you draw down the cash bucket, your total asset allocation will drift more and more toward equities. Adopting the bucketing approach to retirement income planning will affect your total asset allocation, and the implicit exposure to equities will fluctuate over time (as your overall allocation to equities and their higher volatility increases as you empty your cash bucket). Then, if you experience a poor initial sequence of investment returns—so that you have been forced to liquidate all of your cash investment—you might find yourself with 100 percent equity exposure well into retirement, and possibly deep into a bear market. You will have traded *income stability* for *asset instability*. Don't let optical illusions fool you into thinking your retirement income portfolio is safer than it really is.

Would Saving More Save Your Retirement?

In the recent pension debate, some have argued that what Canadians need is more RRSP contribution room. This argument suggests that the current limit on RRSP contributions (18 percent of your earned income, to a maximum of $22,000 in 2010) should be increased, with one proposal suggesting the limit should be nearly doubled to 34 percent of earned income, to a maximum of $42,000. If Canadians could shelter more income from taxation and earn tax-sheltered growth on RRSP investments, the argument goes, our retirement income problems might be solved. If we had a bigger pile of assets from which to draw retirement income, the risks we've just outlined would be diminished (or so the case is made).

However, as appealing as this idea might seem at first glance, the evidence about how Canadians use their existing RRSP contribution room suggests otherwise. In 2008 (the latest year for which data is available), Canadians made a total of $33.3 billion in RRSP contributions—but the total available RRSP room in 2008 was $622.6 billion; meaning that Canadians as a whole used just over 5 percent of the RRSP room available to us. And the median contribution in 2008 was $2,700—slightly lower than the 2007 median of $2,780.

So it is difficult for us to concur that increasing a largely unused benefit of the tax system will genuinely solve the retirement income problems of Canadians. There is no evidence that more than a very small fragment of Canadians will use the expanded benefit—just as a very small fragment fully use the existing benefit. In addition, as we just saw from our exploration of Sally's, Robert's, and David's situations—*putting aside more funds while saving for retirement provides absolutely no guarantee of income security or sufficiency in retirement.*

So how can you protect yourself against sequence of returns risk? As we have touched on, and will continue to explain in this book, pensionization—converting a fraction of your retirement savings to guaranteed lifetime income—allows you to get more from less with your retirement savings. What Canadians need is not more tax-sheltered savings room, but retirement income products and strategies that are aligned with our goals. We will discuss the range of available products in Part II . . . but before we do, there's one more risk we need to explore in the next chapter.

4

Inflation: The Great Money Illusion

By now, you may be wondering when we are going to provide detailed examples of how to pensionize your nest egg and allocate your RRSP and other retirement accounts across the various retirement income products available. But before we are ready to do that, we need to have a conversation about a very fundamental aspect of money itself—inflation. In this chapter, we're going to explore how to ensure your nest egg doesn't rot away in the nest before you spend it.

You've undoubtedly heard the expression "a bird in the hand is worth two in the bush." While this saying probably isn't about inflation, it certainly fits, because a dollar today is worth more than a dollar tomorrow, and both are worth much more than a dollar will be in 20 years. Now, why is this? Because that same dollar you started out with will buy much less over time. Sure, this loss of purchasing power might not be evident on the time scales of weeks, months, or even years, but it definitely becomes evident over decades and over the term of your retirement—possibly 30 or 40 years.

Here's an example. Perhaps you remember what a stamp, a dozen eggs, or a quart of milk cost 20 or 30 years ago. It was a fraction of today's cost, which is essentially all to be blamed on the impact of inflation: it causes money to decay over time, like rotten fish and spoiled eggs. (Okay, we are pushing it.) We have called inflation both the "great money illusion" and the "dragon of decaying dollars." The great illusion we are referring to is the mistaken belief that money retains its value over time - when the reality is that as a result of inflation, the value of money actually decays with time, its value disappearing like puffs of smoke from a dragon's breath.

Exhibit 4.1 displays the annual inflation rate in Canada during the last 60 years, in five-year increments. The first column shows the

Exhibit 4.1: How a Dollar Decays Over Time

Year	Annual Inflation Rate	Percent change from the previous 5 years	How much is my 1950 Dollar Worth?
1950	9.02	35.16%	1.00
1955	0.00	14.63%	0.85
1960	1.29	9.93%	0.77
1965	3.61	7.74%	0.71
1970	1.49	21.56%	0.56
1975	9.32	38.92%	0.34
1980	12.06	52.13%	0.16
1985	4.19	45.69%	0.09
1990	6.22	24.00%	0.07
1995	1.26	12.90%	0.06
2000	2.87	8.00%	0.05
2005	2.18	24.40%	0.04
2010		17.00%	0.03
Average Inflation Rate, 1950-2010:		3.81	

year in question, the second column shows the inflation rate in that year—as measured by the change in the consumer price index (CPI). The third column shows the rate of change from one five-year period to the next, and the final column displays the corrosive impact of inflation on a 1950 dollar (more on this in a moment).

Inflation statistics are collected by Statistics Canada and are also readily available on the Bank of Canada's website and on those of most financial institutions.

You can see from our table that in the year 1980 the inflation rate in Canada was 12 percent, which is about three times the inflation rate in Canada just five years later and double the rate 10 years later. Notice how over just a few years the inflation rate can suddenly increase unexpectedly after periods of relative calm. You can also see how misleading an average rate is. For example, the geometric average inflation rate during the entire period (from 1950 to 2010) was just under 4 percent, but you can see that it ranged as high as 12 percent and as low as zero.

The final column in our exhibit displays the above-mentioned decay process. Had you started with $1 in the year 1950, it would have shrunk in value to $0.77 by the year 1960, to $0.56 by 1970, to $0.16 by 1980, and all the way to $0.03 by 2010. Notice how over a period of 60 years the purchasing power declines by more than 90 percent. Had you put $100, $1,000, or $10,000 dollars in a piggy bank for 60 years, your lump sum at the end would purchase less than 10 percent of what it could have bought when you first socked it away! Although we don't know exactly what the inflation rate will be going forward, there is no reason to believe this decaying process will end any time soon. The Bank of Canada claims they will keep inflation below 2 percent for the foreseeable future, but does a low general inflation rate actually apply to you? Do you trust that the Bank of Canada can fulfill on their mission? Do you trust their definition of inflation? Most importantly, *does that overall inflation number actually apply to you?* More on this later.

What Does This Mean for Retirees?

When you are young, earnings (in the form of salary) tend to keep up with inflation. In all likelihood your wages grow at a positive real (after-inflation) rate over time, so inflation is just not that much of a threat in your working years. And if inflation picks up, you will likely demand a raise, or perhaps a bonus, from your employer to keep up with the cost of living.

But in the area of retirement income planning, things are very different. The relatively low inflation rates we have seen in Canada over the last few years might actually be lulling us into a false sense of security. This is because low numbers can be easily ignored. Yet, over long time horizons the effects of inflation can be deadly to your financial life, especially if you are not compensated for inflation risk and if you don't know your own inflation rate. Yes, one of the main financial risks we face as we age is our unknown and age-specific personal inflation rate.

Let's look at the issue of inflation in retirement income terms. Exhibit 4.2 below, illustrates the impact of even relatively benign inflation rates over long periods of time. Now, we don't know what inflation will be like in the future; this table just gives us some points of comparison.

Here's how to read this exhibit: imagine you are getting a $1,000 pension income cheque every single month of your retirement years but that this cheque is not adjusted for inflation. What this means is that your nominal income stays at $1,000 (that is, the cheque is always made out for $1,000), but its real purchasing power declines steadily with time. So as you age, the same cheque buys you less. The table shows exactly how much $1,000 will buy you in today's dollars, depending on the annual rate of inflation going forward.

Notice that increasing the inflation rate from 2 percent to 4 percent per year will erode the purchasing power of your $1,000

Exhibit 4.2: Inflation: What does a $1,000 Payment *Really* Buy You?

	Inflation (Annual Percentage Rate)			
Year #	**0%**	**1%**	**2%**	**4%**
1	$1,000	$990	$980	$961
5	$1,000	$951	$905	$818
10	$1,000	$905	$819	$670
15	$1,000	$861	$741	$548
20	$1,000	$819	$670	$449
25	$1,000	$779	$606	$367
30	$1,000	$741	$549	$301
35	$1,000	$705	$496	$246

Note: Monthly compounding

by almost 40 percent at the 25-year horizon. (We picked 25 years as it is the median remaining lifespan for a newly retired couple, and a 2 percent to 4 percent inflation rate is arguably a reasonable summary range for inflation.)

So, imagine you bought 1,000 eggs in year one, with each egg costing a year-one dollar. If the real price of eggs remains steady and you have average inflation of 2 percent, then by year 25 you could only buy 606 eggs (assuming inflation for eggs is 2 percent) with your 1,000 dollars. And if inflation hovers around 4 percent, you will be down to 367 eggs. Now, you may personally not care about eggs and would be happy to buy fewer of them over time, but the point is that this analogy applies to everything you consume, from gasoline to plane tickets to prescription medication to pet food.

The CPI-ME and the CPI-YOU

So far, we've only discussed generic inflation rates, but the inflation story gets even more interesting when you include *personal* inflation rates. Although Statistics Canada hasn't done this, in the United States, the Department of Labor has created an entirely new experimental inflation index for the elderly. They call it the CPI-E, and it is meant to better capture the inflation rate unique to Americans aged 62 and older, a group that comprises roughly 17 percent of the U.S. population.

You may be asking yourself why inflation would be different for the elderly. Indeed, how does inflation even get measured? The answer to these questions comes down to spending habits. Boiled down to its essence, statisticians measure inflation partially based on how we spend our money.

Here's how it works: inflation statisticians measure price changes for hundreds of categories and items each month. Some of these items increase in price while others decline or stay the same. The weights placed on the different categories and items in the CPI—that is, how much impact spending on a particular item and any change in that item's price has on the overall CPI—reflect our average spending habits. If the typical Canadian spends three times as much money on banana products as on avocado products, then the index weight placed on bananas is three times as high as the index weight placed on avocados, regardless of your allergy to bananas and love for avocados.

The U.S. consumer price index for urban wage earners and clerical workers (CPI-W) reflects the spending habits of this group, which includes about 32 percent of the U.S. population (and is a continuation of the historical index that was introduced after World War I for use in wage negotiations). In looking at the CPI-W, we can see that working Americans spend about four times more on food and beverages than they do on apparel, and they spend eight times more on housing than they do on recreation, and so on. To make a long story short, in the United States, the relative importance placed on the various sub-components of the consumer price index differs for the regular index (CPI-W) and the elderly index (CPI-E).

For example, medical care has twice the weight in the CPI-E as it does in the CPI-W, because the elderly spend a greater fraction of their income on medical care. Conversely, statisticians have discovered that Americans in their 40s and 50s spend almost three times more on food and alcohol than on medical care. But by the time they reach their late 70s, their food and alcohol expenditure is only a fraction of their medical care expenses. Now, coming back to Canada, our basic medical expenses may be covered, but other important expenses, such as nursing home coverage, prescription medication or extended health care services, are not covered and may be subject to higher-than-average rates of increase.

Does the CPI Measure YOUR Spending?

Although the CPI-E is unique to the United States, the same issues apply anywhere in the world, including Canada. The bottom line is that inflation indices assume a given representative consumer who may not represent you at all. Indeed, researchers in Canada and the United States have found that the generic CPI is not a good measure of price increases faced by individual households, and that a significant proportion of senior households experienced inflation rates considerably higher than the CPI.

How can this be? As we said earlier, in recent years the overall inflation rate has been quite low. But even in this low-inflation environment, the costs of some goods and services have risen. For example, we looked at the one-year price increase for a few goods and services in Canada from February 2009 to January 2010. During this period, costs rose as follows: health and personal care up 3 percent, health care services up 4.5 percent, private transportation up 6.9 percent, cable television and satellite TV services up 7.1 percent, travel services up 8.9 percent, gasoline up 15.3 percent, and accommodation for travellers up 16 percent. The lesson here is that if you hope to retire to a life of leisure, including more recreational travel and time to catch up on your TV watching, while still setting aside funds for health care—be aware that the costs of both essential and non-essential activities may increase even as the *general* price increases are low.

The moral of our inflation story is that it is often higher for retirees. But our point here is *not* that you should add another percentage point to your retirement income inflation projections. The fact that some agencies bother to compute an inflation rate for retirees should remind us that *inflation is personal*. After all, if there is a CPI-E, why not a CPI-ME or a CPI-YOU? Depending on where you live, how you spend your money, how old you are, and even your gender, your personal inflation rate is different than the average. We all have slightly different personal inflation rates based on our spending habits.

A Reality Check for Your Retirement Spending?

The issue of inflation is absolutely critical for retirement income planning, and there are two (and only two) things you can do about the problem of inflation: think in real terms and invest in real products. Let us explain both of these carefully.

First, think in real terms. When you are estimating your needs, make sure to budget in a margin of decay for inflation. If you think you will need $5,000 a month to live on, make sure to increase that by 2 percent to 4 percent next year, and then another 2 percent to 4 percent the year after, and so on. (In fact, we will go over this specifically in Part III, where we provide the Seven Steps to pensionize your own retirement income.)

The same issue applies to investment returns. If you are being promised a return of 5 percent, then make sure to subtract a few percentage points for inflation.

Secondly, invest in real products. In addition to thinking in real terms, you should also invest in products that try to keep up with the cost of living. Some investments are actually indexed to inflation and will pay interest, or dividends based on the Consumer Price Index (CPI). With these products, the greater the inflation rate, the more you are paid. So, for example, if you are promised a real return of 4 percent and inflation is 3 percent, you will get a return of approximately 7 percent (think of Real Return Bonds, inflation-linked annuities, and similar instruments).

There are also some investment products that provide returns that are weakly linked to inflation but don't actually provide payouts in inflation-adjusted terms. These include a diversified portfolio of stocks. With overall inflation, stock returns might increase beyond inflation in the long run, but in the short run there might be substantial dispersion—that is, your returns may bounce around unpredictably and not track inflation at all.

In the end, you may want to use a mix of products to guard against the effects of inflation. You may choose to purchase indexed annuities. However, this is only one way to protect against inflation risk—and keep in mind that your personal rate of inflation may be higher or lower than the indexed increases. Our main point is that you need to be aware of the reality of inflation, the difficulty of predicting inflation over the long term, and the ways in which you might protect yourself from its impact.

What Did We Learn So Far?

We've now reached the end of Part I. What have we learned so far? We reviewed the new risks that emerge from the shadows just as you think your journey to retirement is coming to an end: the Spectre of Longevity Risk, the Serpent of the Sequence of Returns, and the Dragon of Decaying Dollars.

We also discussed, in general terms, ways you can protect yourself against those risks: by investing in products that transfer risk away from your personal balance sheet, and by thinking in real terms. But this advice, while helpful, is too piecemeal to be of much use. What Canadians planning for retirement need is an integrated strategy that brings together the products available to protect against the new risks of retirement and that provides a way to effectively allocate your nest egg among them. This is exactly what we are going to provide in Part II, which brings it all together—building a modern solution that is actually hundreds of years old.

PART TWO

Developing A Sustainable Retirement Solution:

The Modern Approach That Is Hundreds of Years Old

5

Beyond Asset Allocation

Introducing the New Science of Product Allocation

In Part I of this book, we reviewed the new risks you face as you approach retirement. Now that you can see those risks coming, how do you protect yourself against them?

In this part, we outline the new science of product allocation, which will augment asset allocation to guide you through retirement, we explore the true function of pensions, help you calculate your Retirement Sustainability Quotient, and ask the most difficult question you will ever have to answer about your retirement goals. Curious? Dive in!

Product Allocation: New Baskets for Your Nest Egg

So far, we have discussed the decline in pensions and the need for pensionized income. We've told you the new risks you face as you leave the accumulation stage of financial planning and begin to use your assets to fund your retirement. The main take away from the preceding section of the book is that asset allocation, despite its value in the accumulation stage of life, is not sufficient to protect you into and through retirement.

Now, you've already done a lot of work preparing for retirement. Today, if your financial advisor asked you, "How much would you like to allocate to stocks, and how much to bonds?" you'd probably have an answer. If she asked you, "How much would you like to allocate to Canadian stocks, and how much to the United States?" you'd probably have some thoughts on that. And if you were asked, "Would you like to focus on value stocks (like Coca Cola) or growth stocks (like RIM)?" you'd probably have an opinion on that, too.

But what if your advisor asked you, "How much of your retirement nest egg would you like to allocate to annuities? At what age would you like to start to annuitize your wealth? How much pensionized income would you like in retirement—and what's your pension income gap?" Would you know how to answer these questions?

These are not *asset* allocation questions—they are *product* allocation questions.

What is "product allocation"? It is the process of allocating your financial resources to *different kinds of financial products* to protect you against the new risks you face as you transition into and through retirement. Different asset classes—stocks and bonds—have different risk and return characteristics and respond differently to the same economic conditions and cycles. Similarly, different product classes behave differently in the same conditions and protect your financial future from varying sources of risk.

Three Product Silos

Today, you can think about retirement income products as grouped into three silos:

- First, there are traditional mutual funds, stock accounts, and other accumulation-focused accounts, which offer growth potential but no guarantees. Retirement income is generated from these accounts by periodically selling an appropriate number of units. These products are used to protect against inflation risk, with the hope and expectation that your funds will grow faster than inflation. They also preserve liquidity (you can generate income as you need it) and the hope of a financial legacy.

- Secondly, there are products that are designed to provide a lifetime income—including defined benefit pension plans, government-sponsored retirement income programs (principally CPP and OAS), and income annuity products purchased by individuals. These allocations protect against longevity risk, but they come at the cost of complete irreversibility and loss of liquidity. An annuity purchase is a one-way street: once you've allocated funds to an annuity, you can't undo the decision. You could think of anything in this silo as a *lifetime payout income annuity*.
- Finally, there are financially engineered products which fall in between these two silos. These are the modern sequence-of-returns-protected investments, and we will call them *guaranteed lifetime withdrawal benefit* products (GLWBs). These products provide guaranteed income (like an annuity from the second silo) as well as exposure to the stock market (like an account from the first silo). At the most basic level, these are mutual fund portfolios with a guaranteed payout each year. GLWBs are a bit like hybrid cars, which run on both gasoline and electricity, switching as conditions require.

To be clear, these three silos are drawn from the existing universe of retirement income products. The world of retirement income planning is constantly evolving, and we expect new products to enter the retirement income space and new features to be added to existing products. In the next few chapters, we will look at each of these silos in turn to see how they can be used to provide income in retirement. But at a basic level, how are they different?

The Spectrum of Retirement Income Silos

Think of the three silos as three points on a spectrum. At one end of our retirement income product spectrum you can find annuities and DB pensions, which provide guaranteed lifelong income through all market conditions, are perhaps adjusted for inflation, and usually leaving nothing behind when the annuitant dies.

At the other end of the spectrum are non-guaranteed sources of income, such as stocks and mutual funds. These sources of retirement income are typically what people think of as making up their nest egg, and these investments are usually individually held and controlled. In this silo, you may have RRSP, RRIF, TFSA, and non-registered accounts holding mutual funds, exchange-traded funds, and individual shares, as well as bonds, GICs, and more. These investments perform differently in different market conditions, and hence these assets are often carefully allocated across different classes to enhance returns and reduce volatility. But what unifies all the assets in this silo is that their account values are usually not guaranteed and will fluctuate over time. Indeed, in Part I we saw how much a diversified portfolio of financial assets can vary in value, depending on your investing horizon and time frame.

In the middle of that spectrum is the newest arrival on the product horizon: products that fall between non-guaranteed investments and guaranteed investments, and include elements of both. These products typically pay a guaranteed monthly income for life (like an annuity) in addition to maintaining some market exposure. Although there are several different (clunky) acronyms used to refer to these products, we will use the term Guaranteed Lifetime Withdrawal Benefits (GLWB) to refer to all similar products in this silo. GLWBs can be thought of like a pendulum that swings between silos one and three, switching between providing annuitized income and investment growth—depending on market conditions and your income needs. The GLWB pendulum swings from side to side, behaving (one on hand) like an mutual fund and on the other like a life annuity, but never quite catching up to the performance of either. When stock markets are doing well and the GLWB mimics the performance of a mutual fund, it will never quite catch up to the returns earned by the (non-protected) fund because of the higher fees charged for the guarantee. They create a drag of almost 1% in performance that eats into your investment returns. Likewise, when markets are in a funk and stocks are down, the GLWB behaves like an income annuity—but never quite generates the 8%, 9% or even 10% for life that you might have earned from straight pensionization. Of course, the reason for the substandard performance relative to both products is precisely because of the benefit they provide: you get to swing from one to the other based on market conditions. In the language of financial professionals you have been granted an option to select the best of both worlds—but at a price!

Now, each of those product categories provides benefits and trade-offs, and accordingly your funds can be allocated among them instead of relying on only one category. This will enable you to capture the upside potential while minimizing the downside risk.

How Do the Silos Stack Up?

One way to think about the different retirement income investment choices is to compare the extent to which they protect you from the new risks of retirement. These new risks include longevity (the risk of living longer than your money), inflation, and market or sequence of returns risk. How do the three silos protect against each of these risks?

Exhibit 5.1: Three Product Silos: Their Benefits and How They Protect Against Risk

	Protection Against Risks			Benefits		
	Longevity	Inflation	Sequence of Returns	Legacy Value & Liquidity	Sustainability	Growth Potential
Pension Annuities	yes	Yes – if you purchase an indexed annuity	yes	no	yes	no
SWP Account	no	! Only if markets perform well	no	yes	! Only if markets perform well	yes
GLWBs	Yes – but less than an annuity	! Only if markets perform well	yes	Yes – but less than a SWP account	Yes – but less than a SWP account (due to fees)	Yes – but less than a SWP account (due to fees)

You can see from Exhibit 5.1 that there is no one silo that protects against all risks and provides all benefits. As we've said, it intuitively makes sense to spread your nest egg resources across these three product silos—to capture the longevity insurance from annuities, for example, as well as the growth potential from traditional mutual funds.

We're going to examine the benefits and trade-offs in detail, but first we'll look more closely at annuities, the oldest entrant in the retirement income field.

6

An Introduction to Life Annuities

With any luck, our description of the new risks of retirement in the first part of the book didn't alarm you too much and you are actually looking forward to the possibility of 35 years of retirement (or perhaps even longer!). Still, what should cause some apprehension is the chance that your retirement nest egg (your financial capital) will not last as long as you do. Paying for 30 to 40 years of retirement can create quite a burden on you, your portfolio, and perhaps even your children. The good news is that you can *insure* against this kind of risk, and at a very reasonable price.

Now, yes, one normally thinks about buying insurance to protect you if terrible things happen, like your house burning down, or your car getting totalled, or you being paralyzed from an accident, or some other horrible thing like that. But the truth is that these days you can also buy insurance against things that are only kind of bad, including almost anything that might cause you personal stress or economic discomfort. For example, you can buy insurance to protect you against the price of your morning Starbucks coffee doubling next year as a result of a drought in the Ivory Coast, and you can buy insurance to protect your stock portfolio from suffering losses in the market, which can be catastrophic when you are about to retire.

In general, our view on insurance policies—whether they are extended warranties, product replacement plans, or life insurance—is that you should only pay to insure against financially devastating events that can wreak serious havoc on your personal finances. We believe you should not waste money on insurance policies and products that only protect you against financial losses that are relatively minor. (This will vary between individuals and depend on your total resources. If a kidney transplant for your beloved cat will bankrupt you, go ahead and purchase pet insurance from the veterinarian. Otherwise, save the cost of premiums instead.)

Back to our point: as we've demonstrated, longevity risk can potentially ruin your retirement if you don't have a true pension, and longevity insurance can protect you against longevity risk. At first consideration, we agree that it might seem quite odd to buy insurance against a blessing (living a long life), but the insurance doesn't protect you against living a long life—it protects you against the *cost* of this outcome if it materializes. Moreover, this longevity insurance is embedded inside a product that you are already familiar with by now—yes, pensions.

Pension Contributions as Insurance Premiums

Think about how a full and proper pension works. Once you retire, you become entitled to a monthly income that lasts for the rest of your natural life. This pension obviously isn't free to provide. Most likely your employer (if they offer such a pension) will have deducted a few hundred dollars from your paycheque each and every month to fund it. You can think about these deductions as if they are insurance premiums paid to an insurance company while you are working. Then, when you retire, the periodic income a pension generates is your insurance payoff. This payoff usually continues to your spouse if he or she outlives you.

Let's do some basic annuity math to demonstrate how a pension might work (leaving aside inflation, taxes, and other real-world variables for the moment). In the simplest of cases, if you are receiving $1,000 per month from age 65 and you live to age 105, your pension will pay $480,000 over the course of your life (that is, $1,000 per month × 480 months). On the other hand, if you only survive to age 80, the total payout will be $180,000 (or $1,000 per month × 180 months). The basic rule of pension math is: the longer you live, the greater the payoff. Now, given that basic rule, we're suggesting you can think about pensions like your insurance against longevity risk.

As you can see from our discussion so far, a pension has characteristics similar to a bond that pays monthly interest (the pension cheque), in addition to its elements of insurance. Whether your pension behaves more like a bond or more like insurance depends entirely on how long you live. If you don't end up living very long, your pension may act like a bond in your portfolio, in that it simply repays your own money back to you at regular intervals. But if you live longer than expected, your pension will be more like an insurance policy, which not only returns your money but adds more (possibly much more). Just like with your house insurance, if the risk against which you are insuring is realized (you live longer than expected), you receive value from the insurance company that may well exceed the total value of the premiums you paid. This is exactly the protection that pensions provide.

Buying a Personal Pension

So, where do you get your longevity insurance if you don't have a pension from your employer? The answer is that you can buy your own personal pension. It will likely not be called a pension, but a *life annuity*, and, as we've said, that is the term we will use in this book to describe a personal pension.

Now, you might think we are talking about some kind of life insurance—but we aren't. Life insurance (perhaps best understood as premature death insurance) pays off when you die. But the financial products we are thinking about pay off during your lifetime—if you *don't* die. And what distinguishes these products from any other kind of investment product are "mortality credits," or contributions that are reallocated from those who die to those who survive, and which form part of the payments to surviving purchasers.

Before we go any further, please note that we are not advocating you turn all of your cash over to an insurance company to purchase a life annuity. We will discuss how much of your nest egg to invest in annuities later in this part, and then in detail in Part III, but we aren't quite there yet.

Back to annuities. An annuity is actually an ancient product, reaching back to Roman times. Life annuities were paid to Roman soldiers in exchange for their military service, and wealthy Romans could bequeath an income for life to their heirs. Today, anyone can give an insurance company a lump sum in exchange for monthly income for life—no military service or rich relatives required. You can buy a life annuity at retirement with one lump sum payment (this is known as an "immediate annuity"), or you can buy annuities slowly, a few thousand dollars' worth at a time, starting at or before retirement (these are immediate annuities purchased over time). Finally, you can buy annuities at or before retirement and elect to start receiving payments later (this is a "deferred income annuity").

If you are interested in purchasing an annuity, you can get quotes (different insurance companies will pay out at different rates) and compare your alternatives. You can also purchase many different riders that will affect the payout you will receive, including riders to provide inflation protection, cost of living increases, and guaranteed payout periods (i.e., you are guaranteed to receive payments for a set period, whether you are living or not). You can also buy term annuities (for a specified term, not a lifetime annuity), joint annuities that pay out as long as one member of a couple is alive, and so on. Individual annuities can be bought with registered funds from individual RRSPs, locked-in RRSPs, defined contribution pension plans, or deferred profit sharing plans. Annuities can also be purchased with "after-tax" (non-registered) funds. In addition, when you are buying an annuity, you can choose between options that affect how the payments are taxed.

In sum, there's a lot to consider if you are contemplating purchasing an annuity. But right now, we're just thinking and talking about annuities at a very basic level and in contrast to the other retirement income product silos. No need to worry about the specific annuity you might want, yet.

Converting Your Nest Egg to Retirement Income

Remember our three savers, Sally, Robert, and David? Let's bring the discussion of their savings directly into retirement income terms.

Recall that Sally saved for retirement using T-bills, Robert invested exclusively in Canadian equities, and David adopted a more diversified strategy, investing in Canadian equities with 75 percent of his contributions and U.S. equities with the other 25 percent.

Take a look at the table in Exhibit 6.1. This table shows how much you might have as annuity income if you invested like Sally, Robert, or David—and then bought a life annuity with your savings. Depending on which saving strategy you followed, whether you are male or female, when you decided to start saving, and when you decided to retire—you might end up with as little as $1,200 in monthly income or as much as $2,500. (We've already said that women need to plan for a longer retirement, which is why women can expect lower annuity payments for the same lump sum investment, as they have a longer expected lifespan.)

Exhibit 6.1: How Much Monthly Income?

Annuity Payout for 65-year-old Based on Returns after 15 Years of $1,000 Monthly Saving = $ 180,000 Invested

	T-Bill		S&P/TSX		75% TSX, 25% S&P500	
Retire at the end of . . .	**Male**	**Female**	**Male**	**Female**	**Male**	**Female**
March '10	$1,531	$1,382	$1,853	$1,673	$1,620	$1,463
May '09	$1,621	$1,468	$1,611	$1,459	$1,447	$1,310
July '08	$1,600	$1,435	$2,517	$2,257	$2,138	$1,917

Source: CANNEX Financial Exchanges Limited.

We highlighted the highest value for each strategy in Exhibit 6.1. Remember, each of our savers socked away the same amount—but (looking at the July 2008 retirement date, for example) a saver with one strategy could end up with a monthly payment of $1,000 more than another saver who puts aside the *same amount of money over the same number of years*. Moreover, the extra risk Robert and David assumed (compared to Sally) provided absolutely no guarantee of enhanced retirement income: the results of the T-bill strategy were, in our view, much too close for comfort to those of the equity-based strategies. (Now, this is not an argument against stock market investing. Instead, our point is that leaving your retirement income prospects entirely up to the stock market is a risky strategy!)

When Should You Buy an Annuity?

Okay. If you think you'd like a self-purchased pension in retirement, when should you buy it? Recall that we said you can buy annuities right when you retire (or later) and start receiving payment immediately (an immediate annuity), or you can buy annuities before retirement, even well before retirement, and start receiving payment at retirement or later (a deferred annuity). Exhibit 6.2 shows some sample prices for immediate and deferred annuities purchased at ages 35, 50, and 65, and with payouts starting at ages 65, 75, and 85.

What you can see from this table is that for $1,000 of monthly income you will pay vastly different amounts, depending on both your age at the time of purchase and your age at the time the payouts start. For example, the same $1,000 per month of income costs about four times as much if you purchase it at age 65, not age 35. Alternately, if you delay your payout to age 75 or 85, the cost of your monthly $1,000 goes way down. The most expensive choice from the nine listed in the table is to purchase an immediate annuity at age 65. Delaying either your purchase or your payouts to an older age reduces the cost considerably. And why is that? First, the same amount of yearly income, received over a shorter period of time, costs less. And secondly, as you age, more people born in the same year as you die, meaning the mortality credits increase over time.

Now, just to be perfectly honest here, we didn't get the numbers in Exhibit 6.2 from an insurance company. These numbers change from day to day, depending on market conditions such as interest

Exhibit 6.2: Lump Sum Cost of Immediate and Deferred Annuity Payouts

	Lump Sum cost of $1,000 per month of annuity income starting at age . . .		
Age at which you buy the annuity	**65**	**75**	**85**
35	45,390	19,180	5,368
50	83,757	35,392	9,905
65	162,259	68,563	19,189

Source: QWeMA Group Calculations.

rates. Rather, we used the pricing models that insurance actuaries themselves use to compute and then offer these life annuities. Moreover, the price will be different, depending on the specific bells and whistles you might want added to your life annuity—for example, a guarantee that your children will get some residual value, or perhaps that your spouse can continue the income when you die.

To contrast with the information in Exhibit 6.2, we also collected the historical price of $1,000 of monthly income for life, starting at age 65, over the last 10 years in Canada.

Exhibit 6.3 : Cost of $1,000 in Monthly Lifetime Annuity Income, Starting at Age 65

Year	Female	Male
2010	$161,829	$146,415
2009	$161,611	$146,252
2008	$168,749	$151,382
2007	$173,536	$155,458
2006	$173,254	$155,231
2005	$164,895	$148,006
2004	$158,854	$142,463
2003	$151,709	$135,960
2002	$146,281	$131,576
2001	$145,693	$131,033
Average	$160,641	$144,378

Source: CANNEX Financial Exchanges Limited for non-indexed annuity income from age 65 purchased in a registered plan with no guarantee period. Value based on average of top 5 quotes.

What you can see from Exhibit 6.3 is that the cost of the same amount of annuity income has changed over time. Why do you think this might be?

There are a number of reasons why annuity prices change, because a variety of factors affect how annuities are priced. These factors include changes in interest rates and in the "yield curve" (which is a graph that illustrates the relationship between yield and maturity among similar fixed income securities). Increases in Canadian longevity—how long people are living—also affect annuity prices. Over time, as longevity increases and fewer people die at any given age, the amount of money available to redistribute to survivors is reduced. "Adverse selection," or the phenomenon of healthier-than-average people buying annuities compared to the population as a whole, causes issuers to adjust annuity prices as they attempt to match the longevity of purchasers with the annuity products purchased. Finally, changes in competitiveness and competition in the insurance marketplace also influence how much a purchaser will pay for lifetime annuity income. All of these factors influence how much an annuity will cost for people in the same position, but buying at different times. And there's still more to the annuity payout story, in the form of mortality credits—which we'll get to shortly.

Annuities versus GICs

Some readers might think that our description of a life annuity sounds and looks awfully like a corporate bond, bank term deposit, or a guaranteed investment certificate. That is, with both an annuity and a GIC you give a financial company a lump sum in exchange for regular distributions of income. And while it is true there are similarities between these instruments—in that you pay something today in exchange for some interest income in the future—there are also some very important differences between conventional interest-bearing instruments and these insurance products. (In fact, if you are familiar with payout rates for these types of conventional instruments, you will have noticed this in Exhibits 6.2 and 6.3.)

How so? Let's say your remaining life expectancy is 30 years and you want to provide income for yourself over that period. If you tried to purchase a bond that pays you $1,000 per month for 30 years, you would actually need to pay *much more* than the costs listed in Exhibit 6.2. Stated another way, your investment return is actually much greater with the annuity than with the bond—as long as you are alive. For example, in today's economic environment, a GIC of $100,000 might pay 2 or 3 percent interest per year - while an annuity might pay 7, 8, 9 or even 10 percent, depending on how old you are. But you have to give something up if you don't survive, and what you give up with an annuity is the funds you used to purchase it: as we've said, the annuity purchase decision is a one-way street. Moreover, the type of life annuity you see in Exhibit 6.2 is illiquid and can't be cashed (ever). Remember that *all you get is income*—there is nothing remaining at the end of your life.

This is one of the main ways in which annuities differ from bonds and GICs. With a bond or GIC, you have lent capital to an institution, which pays it back to you over time, with interest, and you can cancel (or cash out the value of your investment) at any time. With an annuity, there's no cashing-out possibility; there's just income during your lifetime.

Is the Annuity Gamble Worth It?

We understand that most people, and especially retirees, are very hesitant to enter into the gamble of a life annuity and give up the liquidity of their investments—because they fear losing control or believe they can do better with other investment alternatives. (You saw the risks of this strategy earlier with our Robert, David, and Sally examples.)

Oddly enough though, when people within a traditional DB pension plan are coaxed to switch into a money-purchase DC pension plan and give up the implicit life annuity, most turn the offer down (and others react litigiously—and even violently). That is, many people appreciate having a guaranteed lifetime income as opposed to a potentially larger lump sum at the end of life—and this finding is consistent with our mention of the life-cycle model in Chapter 1, where we discovered the true value of pensions.

Now, remember that we are not advocating that retirees give up all of their retirement savings and purchase a life annuity. But if you are among those who are a little apprehensive at the thought of purchasing annuities with your retirement savings, let's explore, in more careful detail, the nature of the trade-off between retaining your investments, their market risk, and your longevity risk, versus turning your savings over to an insurance company that provides you with an annuity. We will do this with the help of a story that might sound rather odd, but please suspend your disbelief for a few minutes. The story we are about to tell has actually become rather famous in retirement planning circles.

Great-Grandma's Gamble

Imagine a 95-year-old grandmother (or great-grandmother, by now) who loves playing bridge with her four best friends on Sundays. Coincidentally, all five of them are exactly 95 years old, are quite healthy, and have been retired—and playing bridge—for 30 years. Recently, however, this game has become a little tiresome, so one of the ladies has decided to juice up the group's activities. Last time they met, she proposed they each take $100 out of their purses and put the money on the kitchen table. "Whoever survives to the end of the year gets to split the $500," she said. "If you don't make it, you forfeit the money. And one more thing—*don't tell the kids*."

Yes, this is odd, but you will see our point in a moment.

All of the others thought this was an interesting proposal and agreed, but they felt it was risky to keep $500 on the kitchen table for a whole year. So, the five of them decided to put the money in a local bank's one-year certificate of deposit, which was paying 5 percent interest for the year.

So, what will happen next year? According to statistics compiled by actuaries at Statistics Canada (something we looked at earlier), there is a 20 percent chance that any given member of Great-Grandma's bridge club will pass on to the next world during the coming year. This, in turn, implies an 80 percent chance of survival. And, while virtually anything can happen during the next 12 months of waiting—actually, there are 120 combinations, believe it or not—the odds imply that *on average* four of the members will survive to split the $525 pot ($500 from the $100 allotments plus 5 percent interest, or $25, from the bank) at year-end.

Note that each survivor will get $131.25 in exchange for her original investment of $100. The 31.25 percent investment return contains 5 percent of the bank's money and a healthy 26.25 percent of "mortality credits." These credits represent the capital and interest *lost* by the deceased and *gained* by the survivors. Exhibit 6.4 shows how the funds are distributed initially and at the end of one year.

Exhibit 6.4: Great-Grandma's Bridge-Table Bet—How Is the Money Allocated?

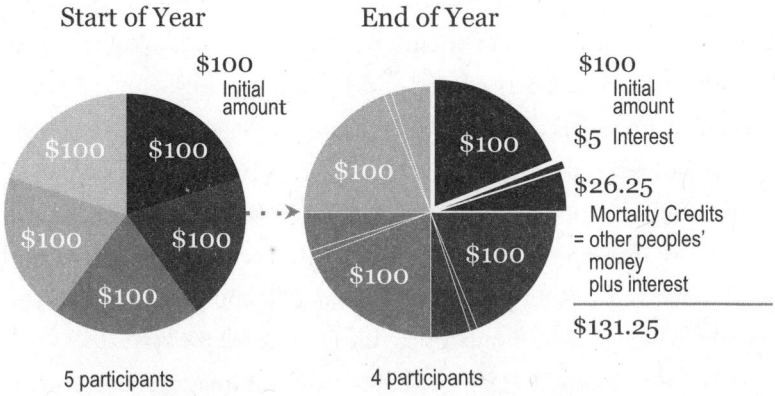

As you can see, the non-survivor forfeited her claim to the funds. (This is the reason that Great-Grandma's friend warned the others not to tell the kids—because the original capital is lost, not retained by the estate.) While the beneficiaries of the non-survivor might be frustrated with the outcome, the survivors get a superior investment return. More importantly, they *all* got to manage their *lifetime income risk* in advance, without having to worry about what the future would bring.

The Power of Mortality Credits

We think (as do many others) that this story does a nice job of translating the benefits of longevity insurance into investment rates of return. Let's be clear about the benefit: there is no other financial product that guarantees such high rates of return, conditional on survival.

In fact, this story can be taken one step further. What if Great-Grandma and her bridge club had decided to invest the $500 in the stock market, or even some risky TSX-based energy fund for the year? Moreover, what happens if this energy fund collapses in value during the year and falls 20 percent—how much will the surviving bridge players lose?

Well, if you are thinking "nothing"—that is absolutely the correct answer. They divide the $400 amongst the surviving four and get their original $100 back.

Such is the power of mortality credits. They *subsidize losses on the downside* and *enhance gains on the upside*. In fact, we would go so far as to say that once you wrap true longevity insurance around a diversified portfolio, the annuitant can actually afford and tolerate more financial risk (you'll find much more on annuitized income, or pensionization, and investment risk in Chapter 9).

Of course, life annuity contracts do not actually work in the way described above. In our example, Great-Grandmother's tontine contract is renewable each year, and the surviving 96-year-olds have the option to take their mortality credits and go home. (A "tontine" is an arrangement for raising capital, and features elements of a group annuity combined with a lottery. It is named for Neapolitan banker Lorenzo de Tonti, who is generally credited with inventing it in France in 1653. Tontines fell out of favour and were ultimately outlawed because the surviving beneficiaries had too much motivation to kill the other survivors, bringing a whole new meaning to the term "mortality credit" . . . but we digress.)

In practice, annuity contracts are for life, not one-year increments, and the mortality credits are spread out and amortized over many years of retirement. But the basic insurance economics underlying the contract are exactly as described above. That is, the investment return from a life annuity—the cash flow you are entitled to—is made up of three things: your money, interest, and other people's money (or mortality credits). And when some participants die and leave their money on the table (so to speak), the remaining participants benefit from those mortality credits—often significantly, especially at advanced ages.

What about 50-Year-Olds? Should They Buy Personal Pensions?

A natural next question to ponder is whether this life-roulette game would yield such high returns at younger ages, and the answer is no. We have created a table that shows the implied return from an annuity at different ages. (We call this an "implied" return because it is not the kind of return you get in the stock market. Instead, as we've explained, the return from an annuity is a mix of interest income and mortality credits.)

Before you look at the table though, be aware that the math professor has taken over authorship of the next section, and you're about to encounter some equations. Don't say we didn't warn you!

Exhibit 6.5: What Is the Expected Investment Return from a One-Year 5% Tontine?

	$1000 Invested at 5%				
Age	End of Year Cash Value	Probability of Dying During Year	Probability of Surviving Entire Year	Cash Payout for Each Survivor	Investment Return for Each Survivor
50	$1,050	3/1000	997/1000	$1050 / 997	**5.32%**
60	$1,050	8/1000	992/1000	$1050 / 992	**5.85%**
70	$1,050	20/1000	980/1000	$1050 / 980	**7.14%**
80	$1,050	55/1000	945/1000	$1050 / 945	**11.11%**
90	$1,050	160/1000	840/1000	$1050 / 840	**25.00%**

Source: QWeMA Group calculations based on Statistics Canada 84-537-XIE Unisex Life Tables.

As you can see from this table, if 1,000 (unisex) 70-year-olds enter into a tontine annuity agreement (like Great-Grandma's bridge-club bet), each contributing $1 at the start of the year, and the entire pool of funds is invested at 5 percent, then at the end of the year there is $1,050 to split amongst the survivors.

According to Statistics Canada, approximately 20 of these 70-year-olds will not make it to their 71st birthday, and accordingly they will forfeit both their $1 investment and any interest it would have generated. So, their money will be distributed amongst the 980 survivors. That leads to $1050/980 = $1.071 per survivor, which is an investment return of 7.14 percent and 2.14 percent (i.e., 214 basis points) better than the 5 percent interest rate available from the bank or credit union—nothing much to write home about.

However, for an 80-year-old, our tontine annuity yields an investment return of 11.11 percent per survivor, and at 90, the rate of return is 25 percent, or a whopping 2,000 basis points more than the interest rate earned by the entire fund. Notice how the return increases with age, so for all of you 30-year-olds out there, don't do this (unless you can pass as a 95-year-old grandmother and mix in with an older crowd. Perhaps book your bridge lessons now?).

What about Interest Rates?

Okay. If 30-year-olds should wait to purchase an annuity, what about 90-year-olds: should they wait, too? We're going to answer this question by looking more closely at how interest rates affect annuity payouts.

An important take away from Exhibit 6.5 is that at older ages the difference, or spread, between the investment return from the tontine annuity and the interest rate earned by the entire fund grows exponentially. It should be apparent from the exhibit that at later ages the underlying (valuation) interest rate (which determines the interest component of the payment you receive) is only a small factor in determining or influencing the outcome.

Thus, it would be silly for a 90-year-old, for example, to say: "I don't want to participate in this tontine annuity because interest rates are quite low right now. I'll wait for a few years until they recover to historical levels."

What's wrong with this delaying strategy? First of all, you can see from our table that by the age of 90 most of the investment return comes from other people's money (the mortality credits). Secondly, if what our fictional 90-year-old cares about is having the greatest amount of income while she is still alive with the least amount of investment risk, the comparable alternative to an annuity—placing the money in a 5 percent term deposit—is much worse! (Again, this argument applies to tontine annuities which are renewed each year, as opposed to life annuities which are locked-up for life, but as we've said, a similar argument for life annuities can be made and is valid.)

Now, there are two important things to note about mortality credits. First, as we've now said several times, once you purchase a life annuity you can no longer cash in or sell the insurance contract. Thus, even though the mortality-adjusted rates of return from an annuity might be very high, it is impossible to separate the mortality credits from the fixed-income instrument. And secondly, it's important to note that in the real world (not Great-Grandma's kitchen) most people buy joint-life annuities, which pay as long as one of the two members of the couple are still living, and which offer some guarantee periods. Both of these features reduce the mortality credits until advanced ages.

In summary: at advanced ages it is very hard to beat the implied longevity yield from a life annuity, and the underlying interest rate (or valuation rate) is only a minor part of the total return. And, as may be obvious by now, the importance of mortality credits increases with the age at which you buy the annuity. If you are interested in computing the implied longevity yield (ILY) for a particular annuity relevant to your situation, please go to the CANNEX website at www.cannex.com and click on the ILY section. In addition to estimating the so-called mortality credits, it will also provide you with some guidance on what your investments must earn if you decide to delay your annuity purchase by a few years. Waiting to pensionize—in hope of getting better rates later on—runs the risk that your money won't earn enough to generate a periodic income and the lump sum needed to purchase the annuity later on. The ILY calculator will tell you what that threshold/benchmark rate actually is.

How Can I Use Annuities to Protect against Inflation?

In Chapter 1, we described an indexed life annuity (one in which payments go up over time because the payment amounts are matched to some index of costs or prices, such as the Consumer Price Index) as the equivalent of a personal pension purchased on the open market.

And in Chapter 4, we reviewed the threat posed by the Dragon of Decaying Dollars—a.k.a. inflation—and how it can ravage retirement income over time. Now, you may be wondering whether you can use annuities to protect yourself against the impacts of inflation.

The answer is yes: one way to protect yourself against the impacts of inflation is to purchase an escalating income annuity. With this type of payout annuity, your payments will be adjusted upward every year by anywhere from 1 percent to 5 percent, depending on your initial request. For example, your first year's payment might be $1,000, while the next year's payment will be $1,010, and so on. This way you can keep up with inflation as long as there are no big surprises or changes to inflation. In fact, if you want *even more* protection from inflation, you could purchase payout annuities that have increases based on the actual inflation rate each year.

Of course, as you might suspect, nothing is free in life, and you will have to pay for these increases by taking a reduced benefit upfront. Thus, although your payments will go up over time, the initial payment will start at a much lower level. The higher the rate at which your payment increases each year, the lower your initial payment will be.

Unique and Personal Insurance

After all that, here's our main message about annuities: personal pensions, or life annuities, provide a unique and peculiar kind of insurance. They are virtually the only insurance policies that people acquire and actually hope to use! While we are all willing to pay for home insurance, disability insurance, and car insurance, we never actually *want* to use the policy. After all, who wants their house to burn down, leg to break, or car to crash? But, the "insurable event" underlying pension annuities (the event that causes the insurance to pay out) is living a long life.

Perhaps this is why the financial services industry has yet to achieve the level of success in marketing and selling these products that it has with other forms of insurance—*it's still too accustomed to scaring us*. In addition, retirees may focus too narrowly on the investment characteristics of an annuity, which makes them seem risky because the payoff depends on an uncertain date of death, rather than focusing on the valuable insurance component of an annuity, which guarantees your capacity to spend over your lifetime. We hope that simple tales like "Great-Grandma's Gamble" can help prospective retirees and their financial advisors understand the benefits, risks, and returns involved with buying longevity insurance.

To be sure, annuities are not a risk-free way to invest. One of the risks annuity purchasers face is related to the solvency, or creditworthiness, of the issuer. (This is also true if you have a DB pension with an employer, as you are exposed to some risk associated with the financial health of the company.) If you are planning on purchasing an annuity, you will probably want to check out the credit rating of the issuing company.

You should also know how annuity payments are insured. Every company issuing annuities in Canada is required to become a member of Assuris. Should an insurance company go bankrupt, Assuris will arrange to transfer its obligations to a solvent insurance company. Even when Confederation Life (a major Canadian life insurance company) was liquidated in 1994, at the end of the process none of the 260,000 individual policyholders lost money. The annuitants continued to receive their income, albeit from the insurance companies that took over their policies. This protection is available to every annuity purchaser at no direct cost and guarantees that if your annuity is transferred to a new company, you will retain up to $2,000 per month or 85 percent of the promised monthly income benefit, whichever is higher.

When you make an annuity purchase decision, you will need to consider many factors—timing of the purchase, what features to add, and which company to buy from. We know we haven't covered all of these issues. Our intention is to provide a basic overview of how annuities work and why you might want to add them to your retirement income plans. Next, we'll run through a brief overview of traditional mutual fund and stock accounts, to see where they fit in the retirement income spectrum.

7

A Review of Traditional Investment Accounts

Reading through this book until now you might have gotten the (wrong) impression that we are not big fans of common stocks, government bonds, mutual funds, and traditional diversification, since we haven't had much (good) to say about them. If you recall, we pointed out how risky they can be and how a run of bad luck with these investments—at the wrong time—can practically ruin your retirement. But does that mean you should avoid them outright? Well, the fact is that nothing could be farther from the truth. Although we haven't yet discussed precisely how conventional investment products fit in a pensionized portfolio, let us make it clear that they should be at the core of a properly structured retirement income plan.

Thus, although we are advocates of product allocation, we don't want to downplay or ignore the importance of traditional asset allocation. And, if we are guilty of downplaying the classical instruments of financial planning, it is because they are ubiquitous, well understood, and widely described by other sources. In other words, we don't want to bore you with something you probably already know.

Recall that the main point we are trying to make in this book is that all current, future, and soon-to-be retirees should allocate their financial (capital) nest egg across *more* than just stocks, bonds, cash, and commodities. No matter how diversified your investments are, diversification and asset allocation are not enough to protect you against the many other risks of retirement.

As you saw in Chapter 5, we believe that retirement wealth should be allocated across three distinct silos. One silo is filled with pension annuities, which we have just discussed at length. For those who are lucky enough to have DB pensions, that silo is most likely covered. For those who are in DC plans, or worse, for those who have no pensions at all—you'll need to get some pension income. Another silo is made up of hybrid retirement income products, a product class we will turn to in the next chapter. The final silo is filled with precisely the conventional instruments, like stocks, bonds, mutual funds, and exchange-traded funds, that you are probably most familiar with from your retirement savings days. In contrast to the other two silos, the income portion from this silo is created by you—not by the product manufacturer, the insurance company, or the bank. Instead, you determine how much you want to withdraw using a systematic withdrawal plan, or SWP. The bottom line from all of our discussions of silos is that to get a perfect retirement income plan you should allocate your nest egg across all three.

Here's our message once again just so it's clear: the SWP portion of your retirement portfolio should contain all the stocks, bonds, cash, mutual funds, exchange-traded funds (ETFs), and other vehicles that you have been using to accumulate wealth during your years of saving for retirement. There's absolutely no reason to stop using these instruments since the benefits of broad diversification and equity ownership remain important over your entire life cycle. So don't fire your stock broker if you pensionize your nest egg—at least not on our account!

Asset Allocation in Your SWP

Now that we've said you should retain all your existing investment vehicles, you may be wondering whether you should retain them in the same proportions and allocations. Here's where we have something more to say. We believe the actual asset allocation within your SWP silo should be more conservative (i.e., have more bonds) during retirement than your normal balanced asset allocation before retirement. So, if your mutual fund or ETF portfolio had 70 percent stocks and 30 percent bonds before retirement, you should probably reduce this to, say, 50 percent stocks and 50 percent bonds as you transition into retirement.

But why do we suggest a more conservative asset allocation in your SWP account in retirement? There are two very important reasons for this. Number one is rather obvious: you are getting older and, hence, you should probably have a more conservative portfolio, all else being equal. That part is straightforward. The second reason, however, is more subtle.

As we've said, we will discuss later on in this part the hybrid investment products that combine the upside of equity markets with some pension-like downside protection. As a general rule, if you use these products, you should ensure the aggressive part of your allocation is covered by the hybrid product. That is, *let the protected (insured) silo take on the risks*, and be more conservative with your naked (unprotected) investments.

For example, imagine you have $600,000 in your nest egg. You want to pensionize some of your assets, and you'd like a 50/50 stock versus bonds asset allocation in the non-pensionized income silos. If you are comfortable using $200,000 to purchase a personal pension or life annuity and would like to split the remaining $400,000 evenly between stocks and bonds, you could do it in the following way: include the safest assets in the SWP component (say $200,000) and then invest the other $200,000 of your equity quota in the hybrid retirement income product. In other words, keep the SWP safe and let the insurance company protect the equities. And, if the insurance company you choose doesn't allow you to have 100 percent of your hybrid retirement income product in equities (and restricts you, let's say, to only $150,000 in our example above)—then take on the maximum allowable equity exposure and allocate $150,000 to bonds and $50,000 to equity in the SWP silo (to keep your overall allocation to 50/50 stocks and bonds).

Some of you might wonder if you should think about the allocation to your pension or annuity silo as if it were a bond; after all, in practice it behaves more like fixed income than a stock or market-based instrument. And that is true to a certain extent, but remember that treating pensions and annuities as bonds, and leaving the discussion there, ignores the many other important aspects of longevity insurance and protection provided by that silo, as we've just reviewed.

In sum: we are not advocating that you be too conservative in the SWP, but that you should think about all three silos together when making your asset allocation decisions.

What Should You Put in the SWP?

The choices of what to put in your SWP account are virtually unlimited, and there are many creative things you can do with the asset allocation inside this account. Some retirees might want to ladder their SWP with bonds that mature at different time periods to create a synthetic income stream.

A "bond ladder" is the name given to a portfolio of bonds with different maturities. Suppose you had $50,000 to invest in bonds. Using this approach, you could buy five different bonds each with a face value of $10,000 (or even 10 bonds each with a face value of

$5,000). Each bond, however, would have a different maturity. One bond might mature in one year, another in three years, and the remaining bonds might mature in five-plus years. Using different maturities helps you reduce the reinvestment risk associated with rolling over maturing bonds into similar fixed-income products all at once. It also helps manage the flow of money, ensuring a steady cash flow throughout the year.

Others might want to include preferred shares with higher promised (although not guaranteed) dividend yields. Some might just rollover GICs as they come due, which is an extremely conservative strategy, and not very tax efficient if the money is sitting outside of an RRSP or RRIF account.

As you can see, there are many possible plans of action for a SWP, and you have substantial flexibility to allocate your assets any way you see fit with this silo. In a very real sense, you have the most flexibility with your SWP compared to the other two retirement product silos. So enjoy the flexibility! This is where asset allocation shines. Just remember our advice to be a bit more conservative with this silo than you might normally like, because the third silo, hybrid retirement income, will take more risk (backed by the insurance company). And we're going to take a closer look at that third silo in the next chapter.

8

Introducing the Third Silo—Guaranteed Lifetime Withdrawal Benefit Products

We have discussed pensions and annuities in considerable detail. We've also provided a brief overview of the non-guaranteed (i.e., stock and bond) silo, which is likely how you've saved for retirement so far. Now we are going to spend a little more time looking at guaranteed lifetime withdrawal benefit (GLWB) products, the least well-known of the three silos.

GLWB products are a relatively new entrant to the retirement income landscape in Canada. First introduced in 2002, they are now available from eight major insurance companies. As we've said, at the most basic level, GLWB products are like a mutual fund (or other non-guaranteed investment), but they also include a rider that ensures the purchaser can receive income from their GLWB for life, no matter how the underlying investments perform.

That is, if you purchase a GLWB for $100,000 with a 5 percent income rider, you are guaranteed to receive $5,000 (non-indexed) per year for the rest of your life—even if the value of your underlying investments goes down, even all the way to zero. While the first versions of these products introduced in Canada typically limited withdrawals to a maximum of 20 years, the current crop provides lifetime income, and most GLWBs provide an income stream of 5 percent of the base amount.

Guarantees and Growth: How GLWBs Work

How do these products work, and how do you know how much money you will get each year? In many ways, these products are like mutual funds—because the products underlying the GLWBs are, in fact, mutual funds. Technically, they are a form of mutual fund known as a segregated fund. A "seg fund" is an investment fund that combines the growth potential of a mutual fund with the security of a life insurance policy. Segregated funds are often referred to as mutual funds with an insurance policy wrapper. Seg funds offer certain guarantees, such as reimbursement of capital upon death, and are purchased through financial advisors. As required by law, these funds are fully segregated from the company's general investment funds, hence their name.

Back to GLWBs. Let's say you invest $100,000 in a GLWB. On the day that you make your purchase, the "contract value" (that is, the market value of your investment) and the "guaranteed withdrawal base" (that is, the amount used to calculate the income payments–also called the GLWB Protected Value) are both $100,000. For the rest of your life, you are now *guaranteed* (like with an annuity) to receive 5 percent (or $5,000) in annual income from your investment. Your annual payment is always calculated from that guaranteed withdrawal base.

But that's just the income side. The money you use to buy your GLWB is invested in mutual funds available from the issuer. This balance is called the contract value and it will fluctuate from day to day, based on the value of the underlying mutual funds. Ordinarily, you might not care about the contract value—after all, your income is calculated based on the guaranteed withdrawal base. However, these

Exhibit 8.1: How a GLWB Reset Works

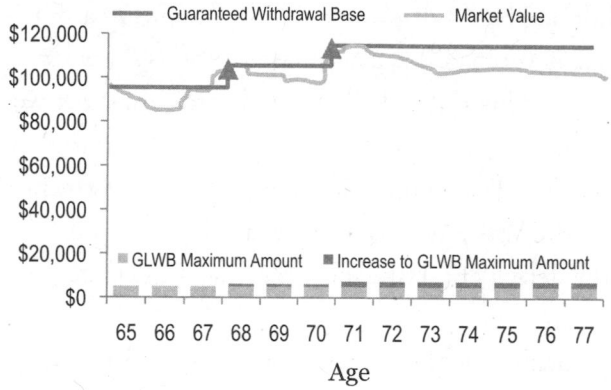

products provide some upside potential if markets rise, and here's how: if your invested funds do well and the contract value exceeds the value of the withdrawal base, then that withdrawal base can be reset to the new, higher level. Most GLWBs allow the withdrawal base to be reset once every three years, and this process is often called a "step up" benefit. We've provided an illustration, in Exhibit 8.1, to show how resets work.

In addition to step up resets, there is yet another way to increase the income you get from a GLWB. Let's say you buy a GLWB product *before* you retire and need the income. What happens then? If you buy a GLWB but delay making withdrawals, then an "income credit" is added to the withdrawal base annually, usually 5 percent. When you begin receiving payments from your GLWB, they will be calculated using the new, higher withdrawal base.

For example, if you purchase a GLWB for $100,000 with a 5 percent (simple) income credit and delay making any withdrawals for two years, the guaranteed withdrawal base will be your original investment + year one's income credits + year two's income credits, or ($100,000) + ($100,000 × 5% = $5,000) + ($100,000 × 5% = $5,000) = $110,000. Your annual payments will be $110,000 × 5 percent = $5,500, not $5,000, because you delayed your withdrawals for two years. And if you delay your withdrawals for five years, your guaranteed withdrawal base will grow to $125,000 and your annual payout will be $6,250 ($125,000 × 5%—note that this is simple, not compound interest). (This is a little like the deferred annuities we discussed earlier, in Chapter 6.) Remember, you benefit from this higher withdrawal regardless of the performance of the investments you hold inside the GLWB. And if your guaranteed withdrawal base is reset during the delay period, the income credit is calculated on that new, stepped-up base.

Exhibit 8.2 provides a table that shows what we've just said, to make sure it's clear.

It's important to note that income credits to the guaranteed withdrawal base are *not* cashable or available to you. You still own the underlying assets in a GLWB and can cash them out if you like, but the income credit does not increase the contract value, only the guaranteed withdrawal base. For this reason, we like to call these "phantom income credits"—because they are not a real, cashable benefit, but (like a phantom) something with no physical reality. For example, if you delay withdrawals as we have just explained, so that you are now withdrawing $6,250 on a guaranteed withdrawal base of $125,000—and

Exhibit 8.2: Delaying Withdrawals from a GLWB with 5% Income Credit (and No Step Ups)

	Start withdrawals immediately	Start withdrawals after two years	Start withdrawals after five years
Guaranteed Withdrawal Base	$100,000	$110,000	$125,000
Annual Payments	$5,000	$5,500	$6,250

then you decide you would like to collapse your GLWB and withdraw all your funds—you will receive the market value of your investment (less costs and fees), *not* the GLWB withdrawal base of $125,000.

At the same time, the value of your portfolio may go down as funds are withdrawn through your regular income payouts, but these withdrawals do not affect the guaranteed withdrawal base—just the contract value. So there are two values which the owner of a GLWB will want to track: the portfolio (or contract) value and the guaranteed withdrawal base.

You can see that these products are a little like annuities because they provide the purchaser with a guaranteed lifetime income stream. They are also like annuities for the issuer, who hopes to benefit by pooling the risks of all the purchasers. That is, those who pay the rider fees finance the income stream for those who exceed average life expectancy and have no money left in their own portfolio values. But unlike annuities, you own the investment assets in your GLWB, which you can withdraw at any time (subject to redemption fees, taxes, and other charges).

We'll look at the costs to pensionize your nest egg using different products in a moment. But how much are the fees for a GLWB? In exchange for the guaranteed income and phantom income credits available through a GLWB, you need to pay higher fees for these products. For a high-equity fund (which, as we've said in Chapter 7, is the best choice for a GLWB), a typical annual fee is about 3.6 percent, and a GLWB with all the available bells and whistles can cost as much as 4.10 percent per year.

GLWBs: Issuers, Features, and Benefits

This table shows you who sells GLWB products in Canada and provides a way to evaluate what we think are the most important features of these products. We have listed the companies by market share—the

Exhibit 8.3: Guaranteed Lifetime Withdrawal Benefits: Issuers, Features, and Benefits

	Manulife Financial	Sun Life Financial	Desjardins Financial Security	Industrial Alliance	Empire Life	Transamerica Life Canada	Great-West Life	SSQ Financial Group
Product	**GIF Select IncomePlus**	**SunWise Elite Plus**	**Helios-GLWB**	**Ecoflextra-Guaranteed Surrender Series**	**Class Plus**	**Five for Life**	**Segregated Funds-Lifetime Income Benefit Option**	**ASTRA Guaranteed Income**
Minimum initial deposit	$25,000	$25,000	$5,000	$25,000	$10,000	$25,000	$25,000	$10,000
Maximum purchase age	80	80	80	80	80	80	91	80
Investment Options (number of funds available)	39	Over 50	15	54	11	23	28	Over 20
Highest allowable equity exposure in funds	70%	70%	75%	80%	100%	70%	70%	70%

Frequency of guaranteed base re-set	3 years	3 years	3 years	3 years	3 years	3 years	3 years	3 years
Withdrawal Rate	5%	5%	4-6%	4-6%	5%	5-5.5%	4-6%	5%
Inflation Protection on GLWB	no	no	no	no	no	no	no	no
Credit rating of entity	AA +	AA–	AA–	A +	A*	BBB	AA	–

Source: Credit Rating from Dominion Bond Rating Service while all other ratings are from Standard & Poor's as at June 2010.

company at the left-hand side of the table has sold the greatest dollar value of GLWBs to date in Canada, with each successive company in the table holding a smaller share of the total market for these products.

You can see from our table that there are a lot of features and considerations to take into account when contemplating the purchase of a GLWB. For example, companies offer different maximum ages for the purchase of a GLWB and different minimum initial purchase amounts. You may be interested in having a lot of investment choice, in having a joint life option, or in maximizing the amount of equity exposure you can include in your GLWB contract. Or perhaps the credit strength of the company providing the guarantee is the most important feature for you.

We are not advocating the purchase of any particular one of these products, or even suggesting any one feature is more important than another. Obviously, if you decide to include a GLWB in your retirement income strategy, you will need to do your own due diligence and work with a financial advisor to choose the product and features that are most important and relevant to you.

At the same time, the GLWB landscape is constantly evolving, with new products, issuers, and features emerging over time. Table 8.3 is intended to allow you to compare various GLWBs from different issuers—but we are not suggesting this matrix is necessarily valid for you or for future GLWB products, or even for the retirement income products that have yet to emerge. We are suggesting GLWBs can fill in an important piece of the retirement income puzzle, and our intention is to get you thinking about how (and if) they can work for you.

In the next section, now that we've gone over the available products for generating retirement income, we are going to start to provide a fundamental theory of retirement income planning. This theory will allow you to bring retirement income products together to build a coherent plan for your future. Ready? Read on.

9

Your Retirement Sustainability: Fundamental Concepts in Retirement Income Planning

We have now reviewed the main categories, or silos, of retirement income in Canada, and we've discussed why you will want to protect yourself against the new risks you face as you approach retirement.

In the coming chapters, we are going to start to tell you how to put it all together, and we are going to take you through a step-by-step process to pensionize your nest egg in Part III. But these last few chapters of Part II set the stage and provide the theoretical background for pensionizing your nest egg.

Accordingly, you might find this to be the toughest part of the book to slog through—but we believe the effort will pay off (literally) for you. To break up the task a bit, as we go along we've provided background and definitions of all the main concepts we're asking you to work through.

In this chapter we are going to start by looking at retirement income planning from a new perspective. In this first section, we want to draw a distinction between financial *economics* and financial *planning*. Now, we are oversimplifying the distinction, but in general terms: a financial economist asks, "What resources do you have?" while a financial planner asks, "What lifestyle do you want?"

As you read through this next section, imagine you can choose from one of two sets of reading glasses to help make the text (and the ideas) clear. On one hand, there are the financial economics glasses, and on the other, there are the financial planning glasses—and we're going to ask you to put on one or the other as we work through this section.

You can see that both the financial economics approach and the financial planning approach agree that pensionization is optimal; they just follow different paths to reach the same conclusion. The financial economics approach is concerned with lifetime resources, constraints, risk aversion, and impatience—while the financial planning approach focuses on goals, dreams, and desires. The economists

Exhibit 9.1: Two Views of Your Finances: Financial Economics versus Financial Planning

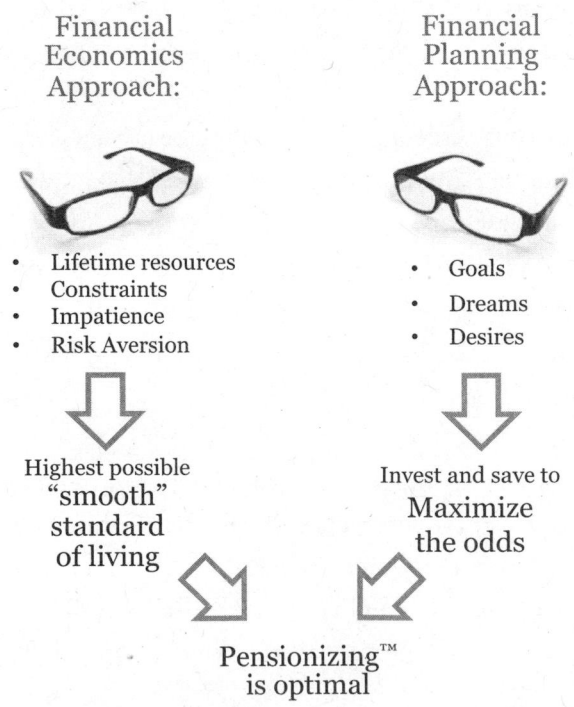

want to smooth your standard of living over time, while the planners want to invest and save to maximize the chance of your investing and retirement success.

Now, this slightly fanciful discussion of reading glasses may seem a bit removed from the practical concern of providing retirement income for life, but stick with it. The implications for structuring your retirement income, and for understanding the role of pensions in your future, are very real!

Which Glasses Will You Wear?

You may recall that in Chapter 1 we described the life-cycle model of consumption, which provides a way to measure the true value of a pension. That is, we said that the true value of a pension can be represented by what people would pay to buy it on the open market.

The life-cycle model also gives us a useful way to think about planning for retirement. At its most basic formulation, life-cycle economics is concerned with how to spread, or smooth, your financial resources and spending over your entire lifetime. According to this framework, during your economically productive years you build up wealth so you can spend it in your old age.

HUMAN CAPITAL AND YOUR PERSONAL BALANCE SHEET

Your personal balance sheet—which is a one-page snapshot that summarizes everything you owe and everything you own—contains two types of assets: visible and invisible.

The visible assets are items like houses, cars, bank accounts, and RRSPs.

The invisible asset is what economists call "human capital." It is the sum total of all the money you will earn in the future

(*continued*)

(after tax). Think of it as the human equivalent of oil and gold reserves that are deep underground and might take years to extract.

Technically, your human capital value is estimated by adding up the present value of the salary, wages, and income you will earn over the course of your entire working life.

This is the value of your human capital—and for many people in the early stages of life, it can be worth millions of dollars.

While you age, work, and save a fraction of your earnings, the value of your human capital declines as the number of years you expect to spend in the labour force goes down. So from a life-cycle point of view, we could define "retirement" as the point at which your human capital is largely depleted, you have stopped generating dividends from it, and you have begun to consume the financial resources you have saved up over time.

How Many Eggs Can You Withdraw from Your Nest?

Viewed in this way, the main challenge of retirement planning is to make sure you have enough resources saved up from the economically productive part of the life cycle (your working years) to spread, or smooth, over the remainder of your lifespan (that is, from the point of retirement until you die). This goal is more difficult than it might sound: as we saw in Part I, simply setting aside money (whether in T-bills, GICs, or a diversified portfolio of stocks and bonds) does not mean it will be there, in real terms, when you need it. So, given that uncertainty, how do you know how much you need to save? How will you know when you've saved enough?

SMOOTHING YOUR LIFETIME CONSUMPTION

Over the years, researchers and scholars in the field of financial economics have developed a set of guidelines outlining how rational individuals should spend their total wealth over their entire lifetime. These are often described as guidelines for "consumption smoothing."

Amongst other things, these guidelines imply that saving a fixed percentage of your income (say 5 percent, 10 percent, or 15 percent) isn't as important as ensuring that your standard of living is relatively stable over time.

So, if saving 10 percent this year will result in a dramatically lower standard of living compared to what you expect to have next year, or the year after, *then don't save*. Instead, focus on maintaining a smooth standard of living—as opposed to a smooth saving rate.

How does this apply to retirement income planning?

When you are setting your retirement income goals and objectives, make sure you are not targeting a standard of living that is much higher than your current (pre-retirement) standard of living. There is no point in starving yourself during your working years just so that your income and lifestyle jumps at retirement. Instead, be realistic. *Smooth your consumption*.

The answers to these questions will depend, not surprisingly, on how much you intend to spend in retirement. And here is where life-cycle thinking can be used to help shed light on planning your spending as you progress through your retirement. Before we go any further, let's take a moment to delve into a discussion on how to generate income from your nest egg in retirement—looking in particular at the concept of safe withdrawal rates.

Retirement planning literature is full of discussions about how much retirees can afford to withdraw from their portfolios each year without unduly drawing down the capital. Many financial advisors (wearing financial planner glasses, naturally) have argued that the maximum initial portfolio withdrawal rate should be in the range of 4 to 5 percent of your nest egg. This is described as the "safe withdrawal rate," and those planning for retirement are cautioned not to exceed it. However, one notable aspect of this discussion is that the safe rate is assumed to be constant over time. Thus the *rate*, not the amount, is the same whether you are 65, 75, or even 85.

But is that really rational? Here's where the life-cycle model steps in. (Financial economist glasses on, please.) Instead of targeting a fixed standard of living or constant portfolio withdrawal rate when you are spreading your resources over your lifetime, you should set aside fewer dollars to be consumed at older ages. Looking at this issue wearing the financial economics glasses, you would be willing to sacrifice income at the age of 100 in exchange for more income at the age of 80, and even more at age 70. And why is that? *Because if you are 70, your probability of surviving to 100 is less than your probability of surviving to age 80.* Thus, giving the ages of 100 and 80 equal weight in your planned spending is illogical—although that's precisely what the notion of a constant safe withdrawal rate suggests. Now, you may be thinking that smoothing your income suggests adopting a constant safe withdrawal rate in retirement. However, relative to pensionizing, we are arguing that a constant withdrawal rate actually wastes resources if you die early. In contrast, an annuity is better at creating a smooth income stream without leaving any leftovers. And more importantly, in the absence of annuities you should smooth consumption—taking into account the probability you will be around to enjoy the consumption.

You will recall that we explored survival probabilities earlier, in Chapter 2, when we showed the chance of living to different ages. What we are saying here is a natural outcome of that first conversation. That is, it makes the most sense to allot more funds to the earlier years of retirement and less to the later years. This has nothing to do with spending less as you age or even with the time value of money—it has to do with rationalizing your planned spending according to the probability you'll be alive to need it!

What Should You Protect Against: Floods or Meteorites?

Here's another analogy in case our message isn't clear: in the constant withdrawal rate model, you are saying you will (plan to) draw down a constant spending level (whether 4 percent of your portfolio or some other rate) in years 1, 2, 3, 4, 5, 10, 20, 30, and so on. This is a little like setting aside two equal amounts of money every year to fix your house—one to be used if the basement floods and the other to be used if the house is hit by a meteor. While both events will require you to use the stored funds, the meteor outcome is so much less likely than the flooded basement that it doesn't make any sense to save as much money to protect yourself against it.

The same rationale applies when planning your spending in old age. Viewed through the financial economics lens, it makes most sense to set aside funds for the most likely outcome (living a few years in retirement), rather than the decreasingly likely outcome (living to a very advanced age). Now, we are not saying—as should be clear from Chapter 2—to completely discount (i.e., not save for) the possibility of living to an advanced age. What we are suggesting is that there is an optimal way to make sure income is available at an advanced age; it has to do with pensions—and we will get to precisely how in just a minute.

Do You Feel Lucky? Pensions, Survival Probabilities, and Spending in Retirement

Now, in addition to the survival probabilities we've just reviewed, how you allocate your resources in retirement will also depend on your personal willingness to tolerate longevity risk. What are we talking about? If you are worried about funding a long life, you will set aside more resources to fund those later years of consumption. However, if you are willing to risk the chance of living a long life, you will set aside fewer resources.

You may recognize the trade-off we've just touched on. This is a variation of the risk-reward conversation you probably had while building your nest egg portfolio. The portfolio version of this conversation is as follows: if you can tolerate more risk (measured as portfolio volatility, or movements up and down in the value of your financial assets), you can invest differently than a risk-averse investor—and you may be rewarded with greater returns. In this case, however, the risk is that you will live to an advanced age (which is perhaps a reward in itself!), and what you are tolerating is not old age itself, but random and unknown life expectancy.

Pensions Change the Game

Okay. We've now laid the groundwork to talk about pensions and the life-cycle model. Everything we've just said about spending in retirement by risk-averse and risk-tolerant retirees is true if you have no pension income. But pension income changes the game—and from the life-cycle view of retirement income planning, *this is the true function of pensions.*

How so? Basically, in retirement, pension income acts as a buffer and allows you to consume more from your nest egg than you would in its absence. So, while you would, with no pension income, be quite worried about living beyond your savings, if you have a sufficiently large pension—or a sufficiently small gap between your pensionized income and your desired spending—the chance of living a longer life should no longer worry you. You have that (pensionized) income stream to fall back on should a long life materialize. As a result, you can deplete your (non-pensionized) wealth (with a higher spending rate) after which you will live on your pension income alone. And remember, if your retirement allocation includes some annuitized income, you will benefit from mortality credits, which will keep replenishing so long as you are alive. (If you have a high planned spending rate, no pension income, and no worries about outliving your savings, you will probably deplete your wealth faster still—but if that were the case, we suspect you would not be reading this book!)

If you have no pension income and you are worried about living a long life, you cannot deplete wealth until some very advanced age, and must draw down your wealth at a much slower rate. And when there is no pension income at all, you can never completely spend your wealth. This is a bigger problem than you think! In the complete absence of pension income, no matter how old you are, you will always be worried about spending too much. In the back of your mind you will be wondering, "What if I have 5, 10, or even 15 years to go?" Taking this logical flow to its extreme, you will never be willing to spend that last dollar.

The overall lesson here is that if you have both pensionized assets and an investment portfolio, then *the greater the amount of pension income, the more you can withdraw from your portfolio in the early years of retirement,* all else being equal. In other words, you can afford to spend more if you have a pension! We'll say it again so it's clear: converting some of your initial nest egg into a stream of lifetime income by pensionizing it increases the amount you can spend at *all* ages, regardless of the exact cost of the pension annuity. Even when interest rates are low and the cost of $1 of lifetime income is high—like now—the net effect is that you can spend more. That is, you can deplete your non-pensionized nest egg, because after it is gone you will have your pensionized income (so long as you have created a sufficient pensionized income stream) to sustain you. You don't need to hold back any funds in reserve.

The retirement income planning take away from all of this is that pension income boosts the amount you can withdraw from your portfolio—and this needs to be considered in evaluating the trade-off between purchasing some pension income versus retaining the funds in your RRSP. We'll get into more detail about how to make that specific trade-off and allocate funds to various retirement income products in a moment. For now, keep in mind: *pensionizing increases your retirement income.*

How Does Pensionization Impact Your Retirement Sustainability Quotient?

This next section is slightly more technical than the rest of this book, and we apologize for this in advance (well, at least one of us does). Nevertheless, we believe it is worth getting through as it provides a bit more mathematical proof for the main argument in this book; namely that you should pensionize a fraction of your nest egg at retirement.

In this section, we are going to introduce some new terms that are key in thinking and talking about retirement income planning. The first concept is the *Retirement Sustainability Quotient*, or RSQ. At the most basic level, creating a retirement income plan involves answering a two-part question: how much money can I spend each year and for how many years can I spend it? The RSQ provides an answer to those questions. You can think of the RSQ like a forecast of your retirement wealth: it calculates how likely it is that your desired standard of living will be sustainable, given the variability of your investments, their expected return, and the variability of your lifespan.

UNDERSTANDING AND MEASURING YOUR RETIREMENT SUSTAINABILITY QUOTIENT

The Retirement Sustainability Quotient (RSQ) summarizes the likelihood that your current retirement income plan will last as long as you do.

The RSQ—which can be thought of as analagous to calculating the probability of precipitation on a given day—is estimated using an algorithm that takes into account many factors, including longevity tables and economic conditions, as well as personal factors like age, gender, health, and whether you have a defined benefit (DB) pension or just a savings plan (such as a DC plan or an RRSP).

An RSQ value can range from 100 percent (very sustainable, and very good) to 0 percent (very unsustainable, and very bad). But unlike a bad weather forecast, you can actually do something about a bad RSQ value: you can change your asset and product allocation to improve your RSQ. And more importantly, *by pensionizing a fraction of your nest egg you can improve and increase your RSQ.* There are many ways or methods for computing your plan's Retirement Sustainability Quotient (RSQ) just like there are many different ways to calculate the economic health of a country, for example Gross National Product (GNP), Gross Domestic Product (GDP), infant mortality rate, life expectancy at birth or the strength of its currency. No particular method is best or superior amongst economists and the same applies to RSQ calculations. However, our preferred method—and the approach we take through the entire book—can be expressed as follows:

$$RSQ = (\text{Fraction of Income that is Pensionized}) + (\text{Fraction of Income that is NOT Pensionized}) \times (1 - \text{Portfolio's Probability of Ruin})$$

(*continued*)

Notice that all else being equal, the greater the fraction of your income that is pensionized, the higher is your RSQ. Likewise the lower the ruin probability on the investment portfolio, the higher (and better) the RSQ score. Notice also that when the entire income is from pensionized sources, the RSQ is 100% and when the entire income is from non-pensionized sources the RSQ is 100% minus the probability of ruin (which is actually a proper probability).

So, for example, if 20% of your desired retirement income is coming from a guaranteed pension, and the other 80% is invested in a balanced portfolio (e.g. an RRSP with mutual funds) which has a 30% probability of ruin, then your RSQ would be: $20\% + 80\% \times (100\% - 30\%) = 76\%$. In contrast, if 40% of your desired retirement income is from a pensionized source, and the other 60% is at the mercy of the market, then even if the ruin probability of the portfolio is 35%, the RSQ would be $40\% + 60\% \times (100\% - 35\%) = 79\%$, which is better than 76%.

One question we haven't examined is how—exactly—we get the "ruin probability" of the portfolio. This is the probability that a given spending rate will exhaust the portfolio while you are still alive. This number can be obtained analytically or via simulation. There are many commercial software packages that can do this calculation for you.

Now, there are variations on the themes we have discussed here, but this is the basic math for understanding and computing the RSQ.

Now, it is probably obvious that the sustainability of your income in retirement is also partly a function of your spending levels (as well as your asset performance and your individual lifespan). And even more important than your spending level considered in isolation, is your spending level as a proportion of your total wealth. We have developed a shorthand way of talking about this proportion and refer to it as your *Wealth-to-Needs* ratio (WtN). This ratio simply measures your total investable wealth divided by your real (inflation-adjusted) desired yearly spending. (We'll show you some specific examples in a minute.)

YOUR WEALTH-TO-NEEDS RATIO

The WtN ratio is computed by dividing two very important values into each other. The *numerator* (the upper or first number in your fraction) is the total amount of wealth that you have at retirement, and the *denominator* (the bottom number in your fraction) is the total amount you expect to require each year (or at least early on) during retirement. (Your WtN ratio will change over time, as your overall assets and desired spending change.)

To calculate your WtN ratio, divide your total wealth by the total amount you expect to need each year. If your total wealth is $1,000,000 (for example) and the income you require is $50,000 per year, your WtN ratio is ($1,000,000/$50,000) = 20. If your total wealth is $500,000 and your required income is $25,000, your WtN is also 20 (as $500,000/$25,000 also equals 20). However, if your total wealth is $500,000 and your required income is $50,000, then your WtN ratio is 10.

You can also express your WtN ratio as a percentage. A WtN value of 25 implies a spending rate of 4 percent, while a WtN value of 50 implies a spending rate of 2 percent. (The bigger the WtN ratio, the smaller the spending rate.) You can calculate

(*continued*)

your own spending rate if you have your WtN ratio—the spending rate is simply the inverse of the ratio and is expressed as a percentage.

As you may be starting to see, the larger the WtN ratio (all else being equal) the better your financial situation.

Note that we are not including the value of human capital in this calculation; nor are we including the value of your house, or any other assets that are not intended to provide income in retirement. Remember, we've said you can define retirement as the point at which your stores of human capital are largely depleted, so this is why we aren't including a human capital value in your WtN calculation.

Now that we've introduced and defined the WtN and RSQ concepts, we are going to start to work with them. Exhibit 9.2 displays the retirement sustainability quotient (RSQ) for a generic retiree. We show the same nest egg under two very different retirement plans.

Exhibit 9.2: Nest Eggs, Pensionization, and Your RSQ

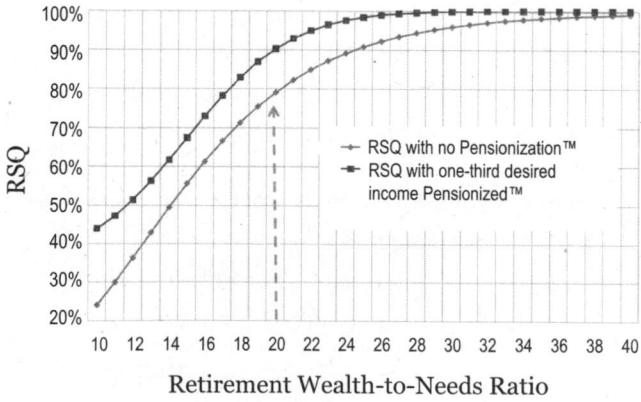

Let's pretend that generic retiree is you. One curve displays the health of your plan if you take our advice and pensionize some of your nest egg. (In the example we're going to use, you have pensionized one-third of the income you desire in retirement.) The other curve shows what happens if you choose to completely ignore us and do not pensionize anything.

Now, before we look at this chart in detail, it's important to note that *you already have a retirement plan* (even if you've never thought about it or written anything down) and a corresponding RSQ, and you also have an existing WtN ratio—even if you've never heard this term before one minute ago.

You might want to take a moment now to give some thought to what your existing WtN and RSQ are. How healthy do you think your current retirement income plans are? We will give you a chance to calculate these numbers later on. For now, we invite you to simply speculate about where you might sit on the exhibit above.

Back to the exhibit. What does it mean? The x-axis (running along the bottom of the chart) represents your real Wealth-to-Needs (WtN) ratio, which we explained earlier. Remember that a WtN value of 20, for example, means that your nest egg is 20 times the amount of inflation-adjusted income you would like to draw each year. The y-axis (running along the left-hand side of the chart) shows the RSQ at different WtN ratios.

Okay. Let's look closely at the chart. Look first at the bottom curve, labelled "RSQ with No Pensionization." As you move from lower (left) to higher (right) values of the WtN ratio, the RSQ value increases from about 20 percent to almost 100 percent. Remember, as you move from left to right, your WtN ratio is increasing—which means you have more money or are spending less.

Our chart shows that if you only have about 10 times your annual needs at retirement and no pensionized income, the sustainability of your plan is a mere 20 percent your retirement plan has an 80 percent chance of failure. But if your nest egg is 40 times larger than your income needs, your plan is virtually 100 percent sustainable (whether you have pensionized income or not).

It should come as no surprise that the more money you have (and the higher your WtN ratio), the more likely it is that your plan will be sustainable. In fact, if you look at the WtN value of exactly 20 on the curve with no pensionized income (which is a 5 percent spending rate) you will see that the RSQ value is approximately 80 percent. Recall that 5 percent is the maximum withdrawal rate recommended by many financial advisors and planners. But if you look at a WtN ratio of 20 with one-third pensionized, you will see that the RSQ increases by a full 10 percentage points—from 80 to 90 percent.

Said another way, two retirees, each with the same-sized nest egg, the same desired income in retirement (so, the same WtN ratio), and an intention to leave the same-sized financial legacy can have very different sustainability ratios. The one who pensionizes one-third of her income wins the sustainability game—even though they are both withdrawing the same amount.

Pension Annuities: Step-by-Step Math

Here is a detailed example to make sure our message is apparent. If you retire with $300,000 and would like $20,000 per year of inflation-adjusted income, then this is a WtN ratio of exactly 15, which is found at the left-hand side of Exhibit 9.2.

If you (our generic retiree) pensionize $100,000 of your nest egg, you will be entitled to $6,000 of annual pensionized (annuity) income, inflation-adjusted and guaranteed for life. The other $200,000 would be used to try to generate the remaining ($20K − $6K =) $14,000 of desired income.

So, one-third of your desired $20,000 is assured 100 percent sustainability (as it has been pensionized). The other $14,000 must be generated from your remaining $200,000—and this spending ratio (which represents a WtN ratio of 14) only has a 50 percent sustainability value on its own, which you can see on Exhibit 9.2.

When you combine the two values as follows: (14,000/20,000)(50%) + (6,000/20,000)(100%), you arrive at the RSQ value of 65 percent. Here is the bottom line. By pensionizing one-third of the income you want in retirement, the RSQ value increases from 55 percent (with no pensionization) to 65 percent (with one-third pensionization). Why? Because you have moved money from a non-longevity-insured silo to a longevity-insured one, *which increases sustainability*.

Is an RSQ of 65 percent good enough? Well, it is certainly better than 50 percent. But it is well below the numbers that would make us comfortable (90 percent to 95 percent). Were this your situation, we would ultimately recommend that you try to rebudget and reduce your spending. But our point here is simply to demonstrate, at a basic level, the benefits of pensionization. We've already argued (earlier in this chapter) that pensions increase spending at all points in retirement. Here we are adding the observation that pensionization also increases *sustainability*, as well as income, in retirement. We hope our message is sinking in: pension annuities keep you afloat.

The True Gift of Pensionization

Here's the main message from this section: at very high WtN ratios—when you have a lot of money relative to your income needs—your RSQ values are already close to 100 percent, and pensionization doesn't make much of a difference. (Remember, pensionization will impact the amount of money left as a legacy to your heirs, because pensionization is an irreversible handover of assets to the provider.)

Likewise, on the other side of the chart (at low WtN levels) the RSQ numbers are quite poor, and although pensionization does improve the situation, the numbers are still quite risky, or unsustainable.

Accordingly, the real benefit of pensionization comes in the middle region, where you can take your plan from mediocre 60 percent and 70 percent values up to very safe 90 percent (and beyond) values. This is the true gift of pensionization—it provides increased sustainability all along that middle region (not at the extremes).

Now, a moment ago we touched on the fact that pensionizing affects your financial legacy. In the next chapter, we are going to delve much more deeply into this issue—and help you answer the most difficult question we think you will face in your retirement planning.

10

The Most Difficult Question You Will Ever Have to Answer (About Your Retirement)

Before we launch into our detailed discussion of how to allocate your retirement savings to pensions and other retirement income products, we believe that you have to ask yourself a very difficult question. And more importantly, you have to come up with an answer! Here's the question: *who do you love more, yourself or the kids?* Who is more important: is it you, or is it them?

Yes, of course, we know this is a very awkward subject to contemplate. And rest assured that we would never bring it up were it not for the fact that your optimal course of action is quite sensitive to the answer to this question.

Okay, let us phrase the question in slightly different, more financial, terms. Think of it this way: what is the purpose of the RRSP, investment portfolio, and mutual funds you have worked so diligently to accumulate over your working years? Is this money truly meant to finance your own retirement, or is your intention to leave something for the next generation? On a scale of zero to 100, what percentage of your current assets would you like to bequeath as a legacy to your family and loved ones, and what percentage would you like to spend while you are still alive?

Now, whether you have no kids or a very large and loving family, the answer to this question is by no means obvious or to be taken for granted. You may have many children and grandchildren who are grown-up, self-sufficient, and not in need of any financial assistance from you. Or, let's face it: you may not really like any of them. Alternatively, even if you don't have any children, you may have a favourite charity, association, museum, or library you plan to support.

Once again we ask, "What is truly more important?" Sure, some of you might be tempted to say, "All of the above"—just like our kids (or even you!) when asked which of many options they want for dessert. But the harsh reality of economics is that we can't satisfy everyone. (Back to our financial economics glasses again.)

Now, how do you know what is the right amount to allocate to yourself, your kids, charities, or other financial legacy interests? The truth is, there is no formula for this, and no right answer. We know you may have to grapple with this a bit. Work through some different scenarios and perhaps consult with your spouse or a trusted advisor. At this point, however, you don't need to come up with a final answer. In Part III, when we take you through the steps of pensionizing your nest egg, you will be able to see the trade-offs between increasing and decreasing the amounts you want to allocate to yourself (sustainable income in retirement) and your financial legacy. Right now, we are just inviting you to speculate about the overall division of your retirement wealth between your sustainable retirement income on one hand, and your financial legacy on the other. So, if your answer is 50/50 (you versus them), or 25/75, or 75/25 (or even 100/0 or 0/100), just give it your best shot.

Here's where we're going with this: depending on your preference for one over the other, your entire retirement plan and optimal product allocation will be very different. If, for example, you are willing to sacrifice some of your own spending while you are alive so that you create a financial legacy after you are gone, then the types of products you should be holding revolve around life insurance and other instruments that pay more when you are no longer around, but earn less while you are alive. On the other hand, if you are more concerned about maximizing the amount of sustainable income you can receive during your lifetime, your plan will allocate more assets to annuities and GLWBs, and decrease allocations to life insurance and a SWP account.

Retirement Sustainability or Financial Legacy?

The upshot of this discussion is that your desire for a financial legacy—on a scale of zero to 100—is just as important as your risk aversion or tolerance in determining your asset allocation. Remember how the financial industry (properly) counsels very risk-averse investors to stay away from risky stocks and mutual funds? Well, the exact same thing applies to product allocation in retirement. Those who have no concern for leaving a financial legacy should lean towards pensionization, while those who have a very strong preference for creating a financial legacy and little fear of outliving their assets should not pensionize their nest egg.

Exhibit 10.1 provides a graphical illustration of this trade-off. You must decide where you would like to live on this retirement frontier. You can't be in two places at once, and you can't avoid the frontier. So where would you like to sit? This exhibit is designed to illustrate the variability in product allocation associated with different points along the frontier. So, for example, a retiree who wants to maximize sustainability (in the lower right-hand corner) might have annuities, stocks and bonds - while the retiree who wants to maximize their financial legacy (at the top left) might have only stocks and bonds. We illustrated these different allocations using different shades of grey in our exhibit.

Exhibit 10.1: The Retirement Income Frontier

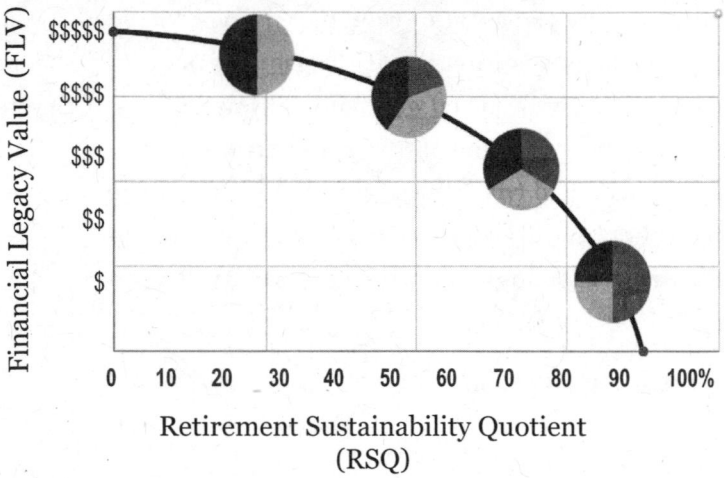

Pricing Your Inheritance

We've just introduced another concept that directly affects your retirement income plans—and that is your *Financial Legacy Value*, or FLV. This value measures, in today's dollars, the financial legacy you can expect to leave from your retirement savings. It is different from a future value, such as an expected death benefit from a life insurance policy. Instead, it measures - in current dollars - the expected value of your financial legacy. The power of this concept is that it allows you to compare your legacy and your nest egg in an apples-to-apples comparison. If your nest egg is $800,000 and your FLV is $400,000, then you know that you are really only using about 50% of your nest egg at any given time to supplement your desired retirement income and your legacy value shows the equivalent of about half of the current amount left.

FINANCIAL LEGACY VALUE

When you die, your family and loved ones and your favourite charity will inherit your assets. These assets make up your financial legacy.

However, it is very hard to predict (when you are alive) exactly what that financial legacy will be (when you pass on). If you live a long time and spend a lot during retirement, you won't leave much—if any—financial legacy.

The Financial Legacy Value (FLV) estimates what that legacy will be in present value terms (that is, what it is worth today). It is generated using an algorithm that takes into account your health, wealth, and desired living standards, amongst other variables.

You can increase your FLV by purchasing life insurance (for the death benefit), by spending less in retirement, perhaps by investing more aggressively for higher returns, or you can shorten your life (not recommended!).

Here is a more specific example to help you understand this trade-off.

Imagine you would really like to leave your favourite grandson $100,000 as an inheritance. One possibility is to just give him the money right now. That will obviously cost you $100,000, but it won't quite achieve your goal of giving him an inheritance, which implies something that occurs at a later date—hopefully much later.

Another possibility is to set aside $40,000 today in a zero-coupon bond that matures in 20 years at a value of $100,000. A zero-coupon bond, as its name indicates, is a bond that pays no interest (that is, you don't receive any payments while you hold the bond) and grows in value over time until it matures at par. If you pay $40,000 for a zero-coupon bond, your favourite grandkid will get $100,000 in 20 years. Now, that might be too long for you (or him) to wait. After all, if you want Johnny to get the cheque when they are reading your final will and testament, buying a zero-coupon bond can misfire on you by decades.

The most efficient way to ensure that Johnny gets $100,000 when you are being lowered into the ground is by going to an insurance company today and buying a single-premium life insurance policy that pays a death benefit of exactly $100,000 to the beneficiary (Johnny) just as you are moving on to a better place. The cost of this policy at the age of 65 is approximately $15,000, which is much less than (the inefficient) $40,000 for a zero-coupon bond and certainly much less than a $100,000 lump sum (if you give him the money today).

Now, bear with us here for a moment.

If Johnny was absolutely certain that he was going to inherit $100,000 from you upon your demise, he could actually go to an investor and sell his inheritance today. Sure, there might be some technicalities since you could change your mind and the investor might not trust you or Johnny, but in theory it would be possible for Johnny to monetize his inheritance right now. And guess how much he could get? Probably the same $15,000 you would have to pay for the insurance policy. Think about it: this is financial economics at work—every plan has a price and every payoff can be quantified.

Thus, the FLV of $100,000 at death is $15,000 today. If you want to leave Johnny $200,000, then the current FLV is $30,000—and any economist will agree.

Finding Your Spot on the Frontier

Let's take this thinking to the next level. If you plan to leave your entire estate—house, car, stable of horses, or RRSP—to Johnny, this too has a Financial Legacy Value today. It might not be as easy to compute as the $100,000 death benefit, because you don't know exactly what you will leave at a random time of death, but it can and should be done.

Now, you may be wondering: how does the Retirement Sustainability Quotient mesh with the Financial Legacy Value? What we have said is that every financial plan has both a *legacy value* and a *sustainability value*. However, as you've noticed, we don't measure both values using the same scale: the RSQ is a percentage value and the FLV is a dollar amount. How do these two values work together?

Perhaps the best way to think about RSQ and FLV is like Fahrenheit and Celsius temperature scales: two different ways of measuring how hot or cold the weather is. And just like someone measuring temperature with both scales, you need to make sure you convert the information you get from one scale so it can be understood using the other.

For example, let's say you have an FLV of $500,000—what is your corresponding RSQ for the plan that gives you this expected FLV? Or let's say you have a plan with an RSQ of 80 percent—what is the FLV value at that sustainability level? Our point is that you need to measure both of these values to get the full picture of where your retirement income plans are going. Looking at only one side of the scale is a little bit like planning with one eye closed. Both the FLV and the RSQ are important values to consider in designing your retirement income plans, and you should really take both into account.

We've already talked in some detail about the RSQ, or sustainability value. Exhibit 10.1 shows us the trade-off between the FLV and the RSQ in pictures. At the lower-right corner are plans with high sustainability but a low Financial Legacy Value. That is, a person with this plan has made the decision (whether deliberately or not) to prioritize sustainability over legacy: more income (while alive) instead of a higher legacy value (at death). In contrast, at the upper-left corner are plans with a high Financial Legacy Value. These people have made the decision to try to maximize the value of assets left to the kids at the expense of sustainability (income during their lifetimes).

What we want to illustrate is that every plan—even yours—falls somewhere on this frontier, whether you know it or not. That is, an RSQ and an FLV can be calculated for whatever plan you come up with. If you have $500,000, plan to retire in good health at age 63,

THE FUNDAMENTAL THEOREM OF RETIREMENT INCOME PLANNING

The Fundamental TRIP states that there is an economic trade-off between sustainability and legacy that can't be arbitraged or violated in a properly functioning capital market.

Once a portfolio has been optimized across products and assets, then the greater the RSQ you desire, the lower the FLV you must accept.

Likewise, if you want a higher FLV, you must accept a lower RSQ.

and want to draw $25,000 from your portfolio each year, an RSQ and FLV can be calculated for you. And if you decide to withdraw more or less from that portfolio, a new FLV and RSQ can be calculated for each of those paths. Depending on how much more or less you plan to withdraw from your portfolio, you will move up or down the legacy/sustainability frontier—the curve in Exhibit 10.1. Travelling *down* the curve (toward the bottom right-hand corner) increases sustainability at the cost of legacy, while travelling *up* the slope (toward the upper left-hand corner) increases legacy at the cost of sustainability. We call this the Fundamental Theorem of Retirement Income Planning (Fundamental TRIP). We're going to look at moving up and down the frontier in much more detail in the next chapter.

Now, we know our discussions of the retirement income frontier are still relatively theoretical at this point. The good news is that we are going to provide you with the tools to make these calculations yourself (later, in Part III). But right now, we are exploring a concept: the trade-off of legacy versus sustainability. Our message is that every plan for your retirement income falls at a specific point on the legacy/sustainability frontier. Don't get stuck someplace you don't want to be!

11

Divvying Up Your Nest Egg

We have now described each of the product silos in turn, and we've given you the theoretical background of the Fundamental Theorem of Retirement Income Planning, which we hope describes the trade-offs between sustainable income in retirement (RSQ) and your Financial Legacy Value (FLV).

Let's take a look at one example in more detail. Take the case of Joe Canuck, age 65, who is trying to determine how much he can spend from his nest egg and what impact the different spending plans will have on sustainability and financial legacy.

Joe initially considers a 7 percent spending rate. That is, he wonders if he can spend $7 per year for every $100 of his current nest egg. Based on where that spending rate places him on the sustainability/legacy frontier, he decides to experiment with a spending rate of $6, and then settles on a spending rate of $5.50 per $100 of nest egg.

Exhibit 11.1 shows the impact of different spending rates on the sustainability of Joe's retirement income plans and on the financial legacy value of each spending rate. You can see that a spending rate of $7 gives him what he considers an unacceptably low RSQ

Exhibit 11.1 Joe Canuck's RSQ and FLV with 3 Spending Rates

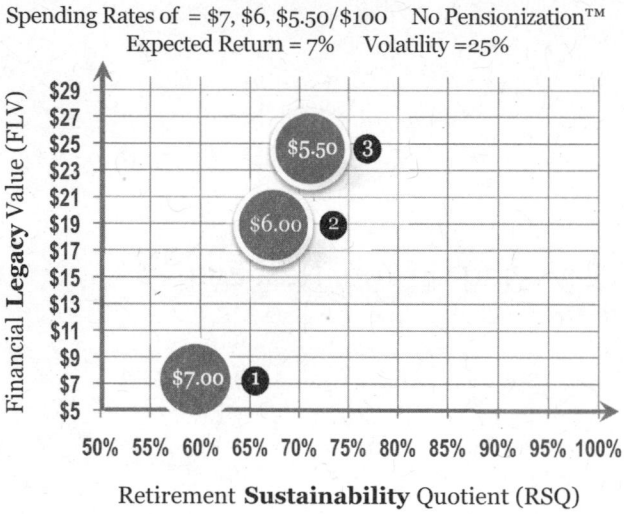

(about 60 percent) coupled with a low FLV (about $7). Moving his spending down to $6 increases his RSQ to just under 70 percent and more than doubles his FLV to just under $20. Finally, shifting spending downward to $5.50 brings his RSQ up to just over 70 percent and his FLV to almost $25. You can see each of these spending plans plotted in Exhibit 11.1—as plans 1, 2, and 3. (You can also see that we have assumed his nest egg has an expected return of 7 percent and a volatility of 25 percent.)

Once Joe has settled (as a starting point) on a spending rate that gives him a baseline sustainability score of about 70 percent, he is ready to explore the impact of pensionization on his plans. Exhibit 11.2 shows how his plans move along the sustainability/legacy frontier if he pensionizes between 10 and 40 percent of his nest egg. Take a look at cases 4 to 10 on the exhibit. You can see that increasing the pensionization of his nest egg increases the sustainability of his retirement income, but at the cost of financial legacy. At one end of the frontier, pensionizing 10 percent of his nest egg increases his sustainability score—it moves from just over 70 percent (in case 3) to

Exhibit 11.2 Joe Canuck's RSQ and FLV with Varying Levels of Pensionization

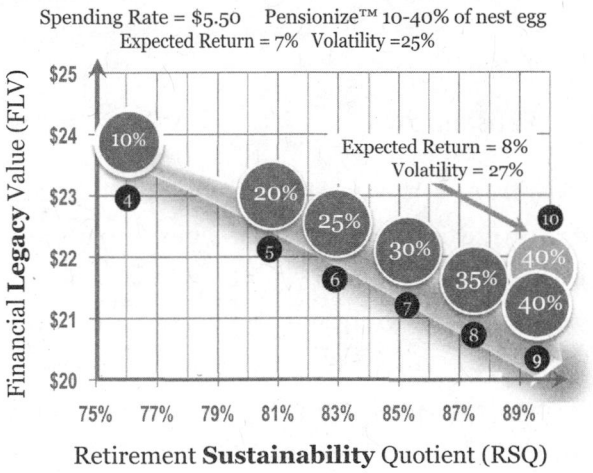

just over 75 percent (in case 4)—while decreasing his financial legacy value only very modestly (from about $24 to about $23). At the other end of the frontier, pensionizing 40 percent of his nest egg moves his sustainability score way up—to just under 90 percent–while decreasing his financial legacy value to just under $22.

You'll note that there is one more case that Joe explores, and it's illustrated as case 10 on our exhibit. In this case, Joe moves up and off the frontier we have traced with cases 4 to 9 by increasing the expected return (and volatility) of his non-pensionized wealth. In case 10, he has continued to pensionize a total of 40 percent of his nest egg. However, because he now has a relatively large fraction of his investable wealth pensionized, he can afford to expose his non-pensionized assets to more investment risk, as he has the pensionized income to fall back on. The impact of moving his remaining assets to a riskier investment allocation (with a higher expected return) is to move him off the retirement income frontier. That is, for the same sustainability score (or at no cost to the sustainability of his income stream), he can have a higher financial legacy value.

Take a few minutes to ponder Joe's paths and plans—we're going to work through a detailed example of pensionizing a nest egg in Part III, next.

What Is the Cost to Pensionize?

One question you may have been wondering about is: "What are the costs to pensionize?" In particular, you may have heard that some investment products are expensive, and you may wonder whether the value of your assets will be significantly eroded by annual fees and costs.

The answer is that every option has costs. We've attempted to display the average annual costs for different types of investment products in Exhibit 11.3. You can see from our chart that some products that we think belong in your retirement income plans have no annual cost, while others charge 360 basis points (that is, 3.60 percent) or more. Now, we want to make sure you understand that although garden-variety income annuities sold by insurance companies do not charge any ongoing management fees and don't have annual management expense ratios, they aren't provided for free as a public service

Exhibit 11.3: The Ongoing Costs to Pensionize

to Canadians. The insurance company makes some profit on them - which means that you are paying for this in the form of lower income. However, once the company has committed or promised to make a certain payment to you, they can't reduce your income or increase any fees for the rest of your life. Contrast that with a mutual fund or segregated fund, where every day can be a new (fee) day. This is why we chose to put the number 0% in the chart for life annuities.

You may notice that at the bottom of our chart we've included the infinite cost of having no idea what you are doing. For us, this gets at what we think is the heart of the real question about costs—not what the annual costs are, but whether or not you are getting value for the fees you pay.

Don't misunderstand us: we think knowing what your costs are is an important part of being an informed investor. However, we don't think investment fees are necessarily a bad thing. The question you should ask yourself, in our view, is: "Am I getting what I want from paying these costs, including a retirement income strategy I am satisfied with?"

We would not counsel you to avoid fees or implement the lowest-cost solutions. Instead, our focus is on ensuring you get a retirement income solution that is keyed to your specific RSQ and FLV desires and delivered in a way that works for you. You may want to take a moment to think about the kind of relationship you want with a financial advisor, if you haven't already answered this question for yourself, as well as the process you'd like to follow in working with an advisor to pensionize your nest egg. In order to buy many of the products discussed within this book, a licensed financial advisor will be required. Canadians should be picky about this decision and should seek out good credentials and referrals—and possibly utilize the "dating services" found on many financial service company websites in Canada.

When Should You Pensionize?

Other questions you may be asking yourself are, "When should I start the process of pensionizing my nest egg? Is this something I do all at once, or can I get into this slowly, dipping one toe in at a time?"

The answer to all of these questions is that pensionizing is a gradual process that takes place between the ages of 50 and 80, and will be weighted more and more to annuities as you age.

In fact, our reason for giving you a lot of the theoretical concepts we went over in this chapter was to help you understand and time the pensionization process. We've told you that your Wealth-to-Needs ratio will change over time and that your RSQ will change as well. In our view, you should start to look at these issues when you are 10 to 15 years away from your desired retirement age, and think carefully about what steps you want to take first, and when.

For example, we've suggested that if you say, "I'm going to stay fully invested in the stock market until my desired retirement age and then I'm going to annuitize everything," then you would be exposing yourself to a number of different risks. These include the risk that your nest egg will fluctuate downward in value just as you want to buy an annuity, and the risk that annuity prices might be at historical lows. We've also suggested that annuity purchases pay out more if you buy them at advanced ages.

In our view, you should use the concepts we've laid out in this part to help you understand where you sit on the retirement income frontier over time. If you find yourself in a spot that's uncomfortable (with an RSQ or WtN ratio that is too low), use the tools of pensionization to move to someplace with a better fit! We suggest you should review your RSQ and FLV values periodically, perhaps as often as every year. In addition, if your circumstances change, your RSQ may change as well. One circumstance you may be worried about is if your investments experience a large decline in value before you retire or in retirement. If you would like to be extra-cautious in planning for retirement but before pensionizing, we suggest you run your RSQ calculations with your current assets - and then again assuming a 20% drop in value. If your RSQ shifts downward dramatically or unacceptably after a market downturn, you may want to take steps to protect your nest egg from market volatility. But the underlying point here is that your RSQ can and will change. We're going to give you the tools to run your own calculations in Part III, so stay tuned.

Summary of Part II

In this chapter, you did most of the heavy lifting to work through the concepts that underlie the argument for pensionizing your nest egg. The basic idea we wanted to explore was that pensionizing—which involves using one of the oldest financial products still in existence, the lifetime payout annuity, increases your retirement income sustainability (which must be traded off against your financial legacy value).

In Part II, we've looked at human capital, your Financial Legacy Value, your Retirement Sustainability Quotient, smoothing your lifetime income, your Wealth-to-Needs ratio, the impact that pensionizing part of your wealth has on the RSQ and FLV, the true value of pensions in pushing the WtN curve higher, and more. We've also explored a set of case studies that demonstrate how you can plot various retirement income plans along the sustainability and legacy frontier. Phew!

As we said, the reason we put you through all of this was in an attempt to ensure you are set up to work through the process of pensionizing your own nest egg effectively—and that's what we'll turn our attention to next.

PART THREE

The Seven Steps to Pensionize Your Nest Egg

12

Step 1: Identify Your Desired Retirement Income

So far, we've given you a couple of different examples of how to create a retirement income for life, but these exercises have been theoretical. Now it's time to roll up your sleeves and pensionize your own nest egg. We'll start wherever you are now—whether you are 10 years away from leaving the workforce and just starting to think about these issues, or right on the cusp of taking that first step into retirement.

We've created an illustration that shows you each of the steps you will need to take to pensionize your nest egg. Exhibit 12.1 shows you all seven steps together—we will go through each of these steps in turn.

Step 1 - Identify Your Desired Retirement Income

Identifying the amount of yearly income you want in retirement is the very first step in the process of pensionizing your nest egg. Now, some people might think this is the most tedious step because it deals

Exhibit 12.1: The Seven Steps to Pensionize Your Nest Egg

1. Identify Your Desired Retirement Income
2. Calculate Your Existing Pensionized Income
3. Determine Your Pension Income Gap
4. Calculate Your Retirement Sustainability Quotient
5. Assess Your Plan: Is It Sustainable?
6. Calculate Your Financial Legacy Value
7. Use Product Allocation to Pensionize™ Your Nest Egg

with day-to-day spending and budgeting. However, you just might find that it's the most exciting step, because this is the step that is most directly in your control.

There are two ways to create an estimate of how much money you will need in retirement: working from the *top down* or from the *ground up*. The top-down method assumes you'll need some fraction of your working-life income in retirement, so the way to calculate income needs using this method is to slice a portion of your existing pre-retirement income off the top, giving you your desired income in retirement. (Some might refer to your income "replacement rate" in retirement and calculate the amount of income you need in retirement as a percentage of your pre-retirement income. That's what we're describing here.) The ground-up method, in contrast, assumes you will build a budget for your retirement needs by starting at zero and adding up your expenses one by one. We'll work through both of these methods, in a moment.

While we were thinking about how you might estimate your expenses in retirement, we took a look at how Canadian households currently spend. Exhibit 12.2 provides some of the largest expenses for average Canadian households.

Exhibit 12.2: Household Spending in Canada

Expense Category	Average Expenditures per Household ($)	Percent of Total Household Expenditures (%)
Food	7,435	10.42
Shelter	14,183	19.87
Household operation	3,345	4.69
Household furnishings & equipment	1,967	2.76
Clothing	2,856	4.00
Transportation	9,722	13.62
Health Care	2,044	2.86
Personal Care	1,189	1.67
Recreation	4,066	5.70
Reading materials & other printed matter	253	0.35
Education	1,179	1.65
Tobacco products & alcoholic beverages	1,495	2.09
Games of chance (net amount)	260	0.36
Miscellaneous	1,075	1.51
Personal income taxes	14,599	20.46
Personal insurance payments & pension contributions	4,023	5.64
Gifts of money and contributions	1,674	2.35
Total Expenditures	$71,364	100%

Source: Statistics Canada CANSIM Table 203-0001.

By the way, you may notice we are talking about household expenses here, not individual expenses. You can use the Seven Steps outlined in this chapter to pensionize individual or household nest eggs—the steps work for both situations, and it's your choice how you calculate your income needs in retirement. If you are married, you can pensionize your individual nest eggs and then add your eggs together, or you can do the calculations for your household as a whole by adding your nest eggs together first. It's the same nest; you just need to decide—one egg or two? Either way, your omelette has to feed two people.

Back to estimating your expenses. The biggest item in most household budgets is income tax, and this will likely be reduced at retirement. As you can see from Exhibit 12.2, the second-biggest expense for average Canadians is shelter. If you've planned so that you will be mortgage-free at, or early in, retirement, that expense will decrease. (But don't forget you'll still have to heat, insure, maintain, and pay taxes and utility bills for that property!)

The third biggest item in the average household's budget is transportation. If part of your transportation costs come from getting yourself to a job and back, you can expect those costs to decrease as well.

Finally, for many households, one of the expense categories while working has likely been putting money aside for retirement, whether in a pension plan, RRSP, or TFSA. This expense will probably end for you at retirement, and you may also downgrade or eliminate any life insurance policies you held while working. Now, you might offset any savings with bigger travel and recreation costs if you plan to "live it up" and increase your overall expenses in retirement—but if you want to use the top-down method, then subtracting a portion of your tax, mortgage, transportation, and retirement savings expenses from your current income is a good place to start in estimating your desired retirement income.

Estimating Your Desired Income from the Top Down

To use this method, you need to determine what fraction of your pre-retirement income you'll need in retirement. But what fraction is appropriate? The target replacement rate in North America is often set at 65 to 75 percent of pre–retirement income for the average worker, while Old Age Security and the Quebec and Canada pension plans are together designed to replace about 40 percent of pre-retirement earnings for the average worker. So, you could just choose an amount between 40 percent and 75 percent of your pre-retirement earnings and stop there. (Lower income households might require more of their pre-retirement income, closer to 100 percent, while higher income households may require less; but every household's situation will be different.)

Another top-down way of answering the question: "How much income is enough in retirement?" is to simply use your current after-tax income. Yes, you will still have to pay tax in retirement, make no mistake! But for most working people, income tax is their largest yearly expense—and when employment stops at retirement, that big expense is reduced (but not eliminated).

Now, as the financial economist might say, your desired income may be way out of line with your lifetime resources, so don't get *too* comfortable yet. And one other note before we go any further: we are asking you to estimate your after-tax desired income. That is, the amount of money you want to be able to spend each month, after taxes are paid. (We're going to deal with tax issues in more detail as we go along.)

Estimating Your Desired Income from the Ground Up

Another way to get an estimate of your expenses in retirement is to build one from the ground up. This method might take a little more work, but it can give you a good picture of what your current expenses are and how they might change in retirement and, hence, a great target income for retirement planning. To estimate your expenses this way, you will need to review your spending for at least a year. Perhaps you already track your spending year by year. If not, pull out your bank and credit card statements, create a list or table (or even a spreadsheet) of your personal spending categories, and add in your actual expenses.

Once your list is complete, you can estimate what expenses you will retain in retirement, where you want to cut back, and where you want to add. You will need a buffer for unexpected expenses and even upgrades, such as car purchases, gifts to children, charitable donations, and travel. Ultimately, this is an exercise about what you want your life to look like in retirement, and you can get as detailed as you like. Remember, we didn't start out this exercise asking you to identify the bare minimum income you would need in retirement—but the *desired* income.

Remember, too, there's probably no "right answer" to this exercise! Instead, the goal is for you to create, at least at this point, a starting point for your planning—not a wish-fulfillment or fantasy budget, but a good estimate of your needs plus some "wiggle room" to allow space for you to do things you enjoy and to handle life's unexpected twists and turns.

As we work through the exercise of pensionizing your nest egg, you will almost certainly revisit the first draft you make at this step. Your desired income will also probably change over time as you change your spending habits, or due to the effects of inflation, which we'll explore in a moment, or even due to the life-cycle economic factors we explored earlier. But right now, the goal is to come up with a starting point number you think you can (literally) live with for planning purposes.

Recap of Step 1

- ✓ The goal of Step 1 is to estimate your desired after-tax income in retirement. Later you will learn whether it is feasible.
- ✓ You can create an estimate by calculating the fraction of your current working income you will need in retirement (the "top-down" method) or by adding up your expected retirement expenses to get a total (the "ground-up" method).
- ✓ Keep in mind that this is a first step in the process of pensionizing your nest egg, and there's no need to get it perfect. You will likely return to this step to refine your estimate later on in the process. So create a place to start and go on to Step 2!

13

Step 2: Estimate Your Existing Pensionized Income

The next step in the process of pensionizing your nest egg is to add up all of your existing pension income.

As we discussed in Part I, practically every Canadian can count on some pensionized income in retirement. Now, recall what we mean by pensionized income—*guaranteed income that lasts for your lifetime*. There are two sources of pensionized income you may be able to count on in retirement: the public pension programs available for all Canadians and benefits from a workplace defined benefit pension. What sources of pensionized income might you already have? To help you answer this question, this section looks first at public pensions and then at private defined benefit pensions.

Exhibit 13.1: The Seven Steps to Pensionize Your Nest Egg: Step 2

1 Identify Your Desired Retirement Income

2 Calculate Your Existing Pensionized Income

3 Determine Your Pension Income Gap

While a comprehensive review of Canada's public pension programs is well beyond the scope of this book, this chapter provides some basic information about these programs—plus guidance about where to go for more.

Canada's Public Pensions

Public pensions in Canada are meant to provide income to older Canadians who have contributed, financially and otherwise, to the growth of this country. These income sources are "pre-pensionized" because they are delivered to individual Canadians as lifetime, inflation-adjusted income—you don't need to do anything to pensionize them.

Canada has several national public retirement income programs. These include the Canada Pension Plan (CPP), Old Age Security (OAS), and the Guaranteed Income Supplement (GIS). If you're employed in Quebec, you likely participate in the Quebec Pension Plan, which replaces the CPP for workers in Quebec and is administered by the Quebec provincial government. Several provinces also offer additional provincial retirement income supplements.

In January 2010, the maximum payments from Q/CPP and OAS plans were as follows:

Exhibit 13.2: Retirement Income from Public Pensions in Canada: Q/CPP and OAS

	Maximum Monthly Benefit	Maximum Yearly Benefit	Average Monthly Benefit	Average Yearly Benefit
CPP	$934	$11,210	$503	$6,031
OAS	$517	$6,204	$489	$5,871

Source: Service Canada website at ServiceCanada.gc.ca.

Old Age Security

Public policy analysts like to refer to Canada's system of retirement income as "tiered." Starting at age 65, Canadians can count on a first tier of pre-pensionized retirement income in the form of the Old Age Security program and its companion program, the Guaranteed Income Supplement.

The goal of Old Age Security is to provide a minimum income to Canadian citizens and legal residents aged 65 and older. OAS income is not dependent on your employment history, and you do not have to be retired to begin collecting it. In fact, even if you have never worked in Canada, you can still receive OAS if you meet certain age and residency requirements. OAS is paid monthly and adjusted quarterly for inflation.

In general, the amount of OAS you will receive is based on the length of time you have lived in Canada—the longer your residency, the larger the benefit. If your other income is above a certain amount, you may be required to repay some or all of the OAS benefit you receive. In 2010, benefits begin to be "clawed back" by the federal government once you have net income (total income less deductions) of about $66,000, and they are fully clawed back (at the rate of $0.15 for every dollar over the net income threshold) once net income reaches approximately $108,000. Today, only about 5 percent of Canadian households have any OAS clawed back, and only 2 percent have the entire amount clawed back—the vast majority of Canadians can expect to receive some OAS income once they turn 65.

The Guaranteed Income Supplement

The Guaranteed Income Supplement provides tax-free income for individuals over the age of 65 who are receiving OAS and who have little or no income from other sources. For married couples, the amount of the benefit is based on both your income and that of your spouse. The GIS is not taxable income, but is only payable if you have little or no other income in retirement. We are not providing much detail on GIS here, as it is only available to the lowest-income households in Canada, who will have very little other income to pensionize.

In addition to the OAS and GIS, there are several additional programs delivered through the public pension system, including CPP for workers who become disabled prior to retirement, an allowance for low-income seniors between the ages of 60 and 65, and more. Because none of these programs is designed to deliver lifetime retirement income, we are not including them in our calculations and discussions here.

The Quebec and Canada Pension Plans

The second tier of pre-pensionized retirement income for Canadians is the Canada Pension Plan (or, if you are in Quebec, the Quebec Pension Plan). In general, your Q/CPP retirement pension replaces about 25 percent of the earnings on which your plan contributions were based—the exact amount depends on how much and for how long you contribute, and can be adjusted based on some other provisions, such as the capacity to "drop-out" low income-earning years from the final calculations.

The full benefit is available at the age of 65, but a reduced benefit can be collected as early as age 60, providing you have substantially stopped working (that is, your earnings from employment must be below the maximum monthly CPP retirement pension for the month before the retirement pension starts and for the month in which the pension starts). Every person who has made at least one payment to the Q/CPP over their working life can expect to receive some income from the program in retirement. Q/CPP pensions are paid monthly and adjusted for inflation every January.

For the purposes of this exercise, we recommend estimating your CPP income as if you are retiring at age 65. You can then adjust your estimate of CPP income up or down if you decide to retire before or after the age of 65—but let's start at the "normal" age of 65.

You may be wondering about the health of the CPP program and whether you can really count on that income in your retirement, especially if your anticipated retirement date is still many years away. Over time, the way the CPP program is funded and administered has undergone some significant changes, and new changes continue to be announced. However, the current set-up—which requires contributions from employers and employees topping out at a total of just under 10 percent—is predicted to be sustainable long into the future.

How Much Will You Receive?

So, how much can you expect to receive in pre-pensionized income in retirement? Just like when you were estimating your desired retirement income in Step 1, there are a couple of ways to create an estimate, from preparing a rough cut to building a detailed summary. However, unlike estimating your income needs in retirement, in this case we know the maximum amount applicable to each of these sources: the only question is what percentage of the maximum you will receive.

Now, you are actually not able to get the maximum benefit from all three public pension programs. We have already described the OAS clawback. In addition, the GIS is reduced by $1 for every $2 of other income, including CPP income. The details with respect to repayments (or "clawbacks") of Old Age Security programs are beyond the scope of this book, but you can calculate the likely impact of any clawbacks using tax software.

There are a couple of ways to get a good estimate of your lifetime income from these programs:

- First, the federal government has committed to mailing out yearly statements of your CPP contributions and estimated pension payable at retirement. You may have a recent statement on file.
- For CPP contributions, you can also request a statement by contacting Service Canada, the federal government's online point of access for government information. Workers in Quebec can request a statement of QPP contributions from their provincial government.
- The Service Canada website also includes an online retirement income calculator that can help you estimate your public pension benefits, including OAS and GIS.
- Finally, you could simply estimate the fraction of the maximum payments you expect to receive in retirement (whether 100 percent or some lesser amount) and work from that assumption.

Keep in mind that you will be calculating the amount of *pre-tax* benefits you receive. Q/CPP payments are fully taxable, while both OAS and GIS are clawed back, depending on how much other income you are receiving. In a few pages, we will delve into a case study that shows you how to take taxes into account, so stay tuned.

Benefits from a Defined Benefit Pension Plan

If you have been a member of a defined benefit (DB) pension plan during your working life, you may be eligible for pension income from that plan when you retire. Calculating the amount of income you will receive from a defined benefit pension plan is perhaps the easiest part of the process of pensionizing your nest egg—because for this step, all the information is in the hands of other people: you just need to get out and find it.

Note that, as we discussed in Chapter 1 (when we looked at what a pension is), we are only dealing with defined benefit pension plans in this step. While a defined contribution pension plan is still called a pension plan for Statistics Canada purposes, it does not provide pensionized income—because there is neither a set amount of pension nor any guarantee about the sustainability of that income over your lifetime. In other words: don't estimate income from a defined contribution plan or a group RRSP in this step!

In addition, you may know that when you contribute to a defined benefit pension plan, you can opt not to receive pensionized income from the plan in retirement. Instead, and especially if you leave a plan before you have earned a full pension benefit, you might opt to commute your plan and invest the funds yourself. If you are going to commute benefits from a pension plan (or if you already have), don't estimate any pensionized income from the lump sum you received, because there is no guaranteed lifetime income generated from these commuted benefits.

So, to calculate the pensionized income you will receive from a DB pension plan for which you are now, or once were, a member, contact the pension administrator and ask for an estimate of your pension income at retirement (remember, we're using 65 as a target retirement date right now) from that plan. If you have more than one plan, make sure you get estimates from each one. When you request an estimate from your pension administrator, you may need to answer questions about your anticipated retirement age or years of service for the purpose of calculating your pension benefits.

Note, as well, whether the benefits include any automatic adjusting for cost-of-living or inflation increases. If your benefits do *not* include automatic increases over time, we suggest you *reduce* the estimated total payable by 25 percent.

What If I'm Worried about the Future of My DB Pension Plan?

After reading Chapter 1, where we discussed DB pension plans reducing or eliminating benefits for retired workers, you may be wondering whether you should somehow incorporate the risk of default for your DB pension plan into your calculations. Here's our thinking: if you suspect or fear your pension plan may reduce or end their payments to you in retirement, leave the plan—if you can (and keep in mind there may be tax implications). That's right, take your money and run. You can build your own pension plan with it. Additionally, if you have reason to believe you need less longevity insurance protection than a defined benefit pension provides, you could commute your pension benefits and take the payout instead.

Note that we are not advocating that civil servants commute their DB pension plans, in part because repurchasing inflation protection would be very expensive, and also because most public servants would not be able to shelter from taxation the full commuted value due to tax limits.

Timing the Retirement Decision

So far, we have not specifically discussed the *timing* of retirement as a factor in pensionizing your nest egg. We have suggested estimating your Q/CPP income as if you were retiring at 65, but you may be eligible for a full, unreduced DB pension before age 65, or you may even be planning to work beyond age 65.

Here's our suggestion: get an estimate of your pension benefits as if you leave the workforce at 65, also known as the "normal retirement age" for many pension and retirement income calculations. While you may retire earlier (or later), part of the work we're doing in these Seven Steps to pensionize your nest egg will help you make that decision. As with Q/CPP benefits, let's start with the default age and adjust it as necessary along the way.

Completing Step 2

You are almost done! To complete this step and calculate your existing pensionized income in retirement, simply add your estimates of your public and private pensionized yearly income in retirement. You should include:

- Your pre-tax estimate of your yearly Q/CPP benefits payable, starting at age 65.
- Your pre-tax estimate of your yearly OAS (and GIS, if any) payable (both only begin at 65).
- Your estimate, from your pension administrator, of the maximum DB pension (if any) you'll be eligible for at age 65. Reduce this maximum by 25 percent if your benefits do not include automatic upward adjustments for cost-of-living increases.

Ta da! You have now completed Step 2 in the process of pensionizing your nest egg: you have the pre-tax values for all your pre-pensionized income.

Recap of Step 2

✓ The goal of Step 2 is to determine the amount of pensionized income you will receive in retirement from public and private sources.

✓ You can get good estimates of your public pension income from the providers—get in touch with Service Canada for an estimate of your CPP, OAS, and GIS income, and contact the Government of Quebec for QPP income.

- ✓ Contact the administrators of your current and past defined benefit pension plans for an estimate of your maximum DB pension income in retirement. Make sure to reduce this maximum by 25 percent if the benefit is not indexed to inflation.
- ✓ Add up all the yearly income from each of these sources to identify your pre-pensionized, pre-tax income in retirement. (We'll take tax into account in the next step.)

14

Step 3: Determine Your Pension Income Gap

Now that you've developed estimates of your desired income in retirement and the pre-pensionized income you can expect to receive in retirement, you are ready to calculate your "pension income gap". This is the gap between the income you can expect in retirement and the income you would like in retirement—and you don't need anything more complicated than basic math skills to calculate it.

But before we get to that basic arithmetic, we need to take a moment to consider the impact of taxes on our calculations here. So far, we've only asked you to estimate your desired after-tax income in retirement.

Exhibit 14.1: The Seven Steps to Pensionize Your Nest Egg: Step 3

2 Calculate Your Existing Pensionized Income

3 Determine Your Pension Income Gap

4 Calculate Your Retirement Sustainability Quotient

Your Average Tax Rate

Let's say you want a certain amount of income each year. You will almost certainly need total income in excess of that amount—because of the income taxes that will be due. Everything you pull out of your tax-sheltered RRSP, for example, will be subject to tax because you've never actually paid income tax on that money (for the most part).

Let's start with a very simple example for a hypothetical retiree who has no CPP, OAS, or GIS income and whose entire nest egg is in tax-sheltered accounts like RRSPs. If he has an average income tax rate of 20 percent, then he will have to withdraw $50,000 from his nest egg to end up with a spendable income of $40,000. The rest of the withdrawn funds will go to Ottawa, his provincial or territorial government, and even his municipal government in the form of taxes, leaving him with $40,000 that he can consume directly.

In order to figure out how much you will need to withdraw from your portfolio to get the after-tax income you want, the first thing you need to do is estimate your average tax rate. This "average tax rate" simply measures the proportion of your yearly income that you pay as tax. It isn't relevant to your actual tax filing in any year, but tells you the amount and proportion of income you can expect to pay in tax. How do you figure out your average tax rate? You simply divide your total tax paid by your total income. In the case we just examined, we know he paid $10,000 in taxes, and we know his gross income is $50,000. His average tax rate is 20%, as 10/50 = .2, or 20%.

Once you know your average tax rate, you can figure out the gross amount you need to withdraw from your portfolio each year (and you can start to take your CPP and other pre-pensionized income into account, which we will do in a minute). So, if you have no other income, how much do you need to withdraw from your portfolio to get your desired after-tax income? Here's the equation you need to solve:

Gross amount = desired annual income / (1 − average tax rate)

We'll provide a specific example of this equation in the next few pages, so you can see how a "real-life" calculation might work.

Your Pension Income Gap

Let's work with the $40,000 of desired after-tax income we mentioned a moment ago. Recall that we said our hypothetical retiree needs $50,000 of pre-tax income to have $40,000 of after-tax income (assuming an average tax rate of 20 percent). Let's continue to assume that all of his funds are in tax-deferred accounts such as RRSPs (that is, he has to pay tax on all withdrawals). Now, let's further assume that our hypothetical retiree has $15,000 of pre-tax CPP and OAS income each year.

We just worked out that he has to withdraw $50,000 from his available wealth each year to receive $40,000 in after-tax income.

How does the $15,000 of CPP and OAS income figure into this requirement? It reduces the amount he has to withdraw to meet his desired income in retirement.

So, to determine your pension income gap, you subtract the pre-tax CPP (or other pensionized) income from the pre-tax withdrawals you require. In this case, we subtract $15,000 from $50,000 to get $35,000: this is our hypothetical retiree's *pension income gap*. Recall that this figure measures the gap between the pensionized income you expect in retirement and the income you would like in retirement.

So, what's your pension income gap? Is it positive or negative? Here are the steps you will need to carry out to calculate your gap:

1. Using the equation we provided, estimate your average tax rate (the ratio of tax paid to total income).
2. Using this rate and your desired after-tax annual income, calculate the gross (before-tax) withdrawals you will need from your retirement portfolio in order to get the after-tax amount you want to receive each year. (In the example we worked through, all wealth is held in registered funds. If you have a mix of registered and taxable accounts, your situation will be more complex.)
3. Subtract the pre-tax, pre-pensionized income you expect to receive in retirement (and added-up in Step 2) from the gross withdrawals you need each year.
4. The resulting number is your pension income gap.

If your number is **negative**, you are done. There is no need for you to pensionize any part of your nest egg—*you already have enough pensionized income to meet your daily spending requirements for the rest of your life.*

But if yours is a positive number (which we suspect it will be for most people!)—*you have a pension gap.* So, what does this mean?

A big number doesn't mean you don't have enough money to retire. Like we said earlier, your pension gap represents the amount of yearly income your personal resources will need to fill each year of your life if you want to maintain the desired income you estimated in Step 1.

Now, you may be thinking, "My number seems pretty large!" But don't panic. *This number doesn't represent a shortfall.* Instead, it tells you the gap between your existing pensionized retirement income sources and your desired income in retirement. So far, we haven't taken any of your other resources into account. We'll be adding those pieces of the puzzle in the next step, which calculates the overall sustainability (or RSQ) of your retirement income plans.

We suggest you continue to work through the Seven Steps using the desired income and resulting pension gap you just identified, even if it's large. You can go back to Step 1 and work through the Seven Steps with a different level of desired income as many times as you like—but we recommend proceeding through the steps with the example you've already started.

Adjusting for Inflation

You may also be thinking, "But the number I calculated as my pension gap is only valid for one year—it's the income I'd want if I was retiring now. In Part I, you emphasized the impact of inflation on retirement income, so shouldn't I be adjusting that number to account for rising prices over time?"

Before we continue, let's clarify how we are thinking about inflation in these calculations. When we asked you (earlier in this part) to estimate your desired income in retirement, we didn't say anything about inflation. In other words, your estimate assumes that today's prices—on which you based your needs—will remain the same throughout your retirement. It assumes that the inflation rate for goods and services will be zero for the next 30 years or so. Rather unrealistic, we're sure you'd agree. True, as we saw in Part I, inflation has averaged less than 3 percent almost every year since 1991—but there is no guarantee that the rate cannot or will not increase. And even at that very low rate, the cost of living will still double in just 20 years, give or take.

Therefore, a better way to deal with long-term planning (given inflation uncertainty) is to budget and state your needs in real, after-inflation terms. Remember our earlier conversation from Part I: think in real terms.

At the same time, you must also project your investment returns in real, after-inflation terms.

Let's explore this in a little more detail. You essentially want to consume "today" dollars for the rest of your life. For example, when you adjust consumption for inflation, that means you will consume your $40,000 of desired income in your 65th year, then $40,000 multiplied by the first year's inflation rate in your 66th year, then $40,000 multiplied by the first and second years' inflation rates in your 67th year, and so on.

However, there is a neat way to keep things in balance. We already know that your public pension income is inflation-adjusted, and we've told you to reduce your expected income from a non-inflation-adjusted DB pension plan to account for the lack of inflation protection.

We also know that when you are filling your pension gap, you will be relying on your private investments, and we'll need to think about and estimate what those investments can earn over the long term (and more on that in the next step).

So here's the balancing trick: when we talk about what your investments can earn, we'll look at returns in after-inflation terms as well, to account for the fact that your needs were expressed in the same framework. In this way, we are comparing inflation-adjusted apples (your desired income) to inflation-adjusted apples (your income from investments). (Remember, we've already adjusted your other income sources for inflation.)

We've now reached the end of Step 3, and you've estimated your pension income gap. Next, we'll start to look at how you are going to fill that gap.

Recap of Step 3

✓ The goal of Step 3 is for you to calculate your yearly pension income gap. In order to do this, you will need to calculate your average tax rate.

- ✓ You calculate your pension income gap by subtracting your pre-tax, pre-pensionized income (from Step 2) from the gross withdrawals required to obtain your desired after-tax income.
- ✓ Your resulting pension income gap *does not* represent a shortfall; it identifies the income gap you need to fill using your other resources.
- ✓ We will take the impact of inflation on your desired income into account by expressing the return you expect on your investments in after-inflation terms. More on this in the next step.

15

Step 4: Calculate Your Retirement Sustainability Quotient

As you have probably already surmised from the discussion so far, your pension gap must be closed (or at least lessened) somehow or your retirement spending plans will not be sustainable.

Accordingly, in this step your savings come into play and it is time to include them in your calculations. To do this, add up the current value of all your retirement accounts. Don't include the value of your house, although it is an asset, unless you plan to sell it to provide retirement income.

What Kind of Eggs Do You Have in Your Nest?

Once you've added up the total value of all your investments, the next step is to figure out what kind of eggs you have to draw on in retirement—so we need to calculate your asset allocation. What do we mean by this? As we discussed in Part II, asset allocation is simply the process of dividing your funds across various broad categories of investment. (We are not actually *allocating* your assets here; instead, we are just looking at how they are already allocated.) Again, to keep things simple, we are only interested in dividing your assets into stocks and bonds.

The reason we look at how your assets are grouped in these categories is so we can better predict how your nest egg as a whole may behave in the future. Specifically, bonds have lower and more stable investment returns than stocks (or, said precisely the opposite way, stocks have higher expected returns and higher volatility than bonds). Your nest egg stock allocation may be to mutual funds, ETFs, pooled funds, or stocks you hold directly. Similarly, your bond allocation may be to mutual funds, ETFs, or bonds and GICs you hold directly. You may even have balanced mutual funds, which hold roughly half stocks and half bonds.

You have a choice here: you can calculate the exact asset allocation of your existing resources and project that allocation over your resources at retirement, or you can select an asset allocation you think is reasonable for your assets at retirement.

To keep things simple, we suggest you choose an asset allocation you think will work for you at retirement, whether 50/50, 60/40, or any other allocation. The point here is not so much to perfectly reflect reality or to precisely predict outcomes; it is to build a workable model. When it comes time to make decisions, working through these questions (whether with precise numbers or not) will equip you with the understanding and tools you need.

Filling the Gap

Now that you've added up your nest egg, it's time to look at how to use it to fill your pension gap. How many years of gap can you fill?

Let's work through a simple example. Assuming you are going to retire tomorrow, if you need $50,000 (pre-tax) per year and your pre-tax, pre-existing pension income is only $20,000, the pension gap of $30,000 must be financed from your nest egg, such as your RRSP, RRIF, TFSA, and other retirement accounts.

Now, if all you have in your nest egg is $30,000, by the process of simple arithmetic you can see that will last you for a year. What will you do for the remaining 20 or 30 years? If all you have is $60,000, then it might last for two years, depending on how the money is invested. And if all you have is $90,000, then this will probably fill the pension gap for about three, or maybe even four years, if you can have your money grow in the meantime. Certainly, after five years there will be no money left to close the pension gap.

But what about if you have $300,000 in your RRSP? Or $600,000? How long will that last and be able to close the pension gap? Will it last for 10 years or 20 years? What if you enter a bear market and experience a negative sequence of returns (something we explained in Part I) soon after you retire? And even if the money lasts for 20 years, is that long enough, given the evidence for longevity you also saw in Part I?

We don't really know the answers to these questions, but recent advances in financial forecasting can give you a pretty good estimate of whether your nest egg can fill your pension gap for as long as you need. Although the detailed mathematics are beyond this book, there is a (free) calculator available on the qwema.ca website that can compute the Retirement Sustainability Quotient (or RSQ) of your financial plan. Like we said in Chapter 9, when we introduced the RSQ, *think of the RSQ as a meteorological forecast for your retirement plans, taking into account that some of your income is already pensionized.*

Exhibit 15.1: The Seven Steps to Pensionize Your Nest Egg: Step 4

3 Determine Your Pension Income Gap

4 Calculate Your Retirement Sustainability Quotient

5 Assess Your Plan: Is It Sustainable?

You can use this calculator to help you complete Step 4 and calculate your RSQ. The calculator on the website requires six ingredients. They are:

1. Your age at retirement (check your birth certificate; tell the truth!).
2. Your desired after-tax income (from Step 1).
3. Your pre-existing, pre-tax pension income (from Step 2).
4. Your average tax rate.
5. The current value of your nest egg at retirement, also known as the value of your retirement accounts.
6. The overall asset allocation of your nest egg.

So how do we calculate the Retirement Sustainability Quotient of your retirement income plan? At a very basic level, your RSQ takes into account your pensionized resources and the assets that can be used to provide income in retirement and assesses how sustainable your income stream is likely to be over your lifetime. That is, the calculator gives the success rate of your retirement income plans, taking into account your age, average tax rate, pre-pensionized income, and other financial resources and their asset allocation.

The output is a number between zero and 100, representing the "degree of success" of your retirement income plan. Here's the first important thing to notice: *the larger the number, the better.*

But why is a larger number better? Here are some simple, extreme examples that should make sense. If your desired retirement income is exactly equal to your pre-existing pension income, then your pension gap is zero and your RSQ is 100 percent (and if your pre-existing pension income is greater than your desired retirement income, your RSQ is more than 100 percent!). Likewise, if you have no pre-existing pension income (not even CPP, OAS, or GIS) and you have no nest egg or savings to fall back on (yes, a very hypothetical situation) then your RSQ is zero. If you are interested in computing legacy and sustainability values for other cases, go to the calculators section of www.qwema.ca to work with other values.

Now, here's the second vital thing to notice about the RSQ calculator: *when you add pensionized income, even though you reduce your nest egg to purchase the pension, your overall RSQ increases.* We saw this in a more technical way in Part II.

In fact, if you purchase a life annuity your RSQ will *increase.* That is, *the overall sustainability of your retirement plan increases as the proportion of your desired income is pensionized.* More pensionized income = higher sustainability! You saw this in some detail in Part II, when we looked at the impact of pensionizing 10 to 40 percent of Joe Canuck's hypothetical nest egg.

Now, this calculator (with six factors) is a rather simple one that doesn't account for all the hybrid products out there; it only looks at your asset allocation. For now (in Step 4) you should get to know your existing RSQ without making any changes to your investments or buying any new financial products.

Keep in mind, as well, that the RSQ is not a measure of the *adequacy* of your retirement income—you established the answer to the question, "How much is enough?" in Step 1. Instead, it is a measure of how *sustainable* your current plans are, given some critical inputs—your age, your existing financial resources, and how those resources are currently invested.

For now, there are two things to remember:

1. The higher the RSQ, the better.
2. Adding more pensionized income increases your RSQ!

Recap of Step 4

- ✓ The goal of Step 4 is to calculate the Retirement Sustainability Quotient (RSQ) of your current plans.
- ✓ There are six ingredients required to calculate your RSQ: your age, desired spending, average tax rate, pre-pensionized income in retirement, the value of your nest egg at retirement, and the investment asset allocation of your nest egg.

16

Step 5: Assess Your Plan: Is It Sustainable?

So, you now have an RSQ number. It could be 45, 78, 94 (touchdown!). But what does it mean and what do you do with it? What is a good number? What is a bad number? The way to think about measuring the sustainability of your retirement using the RSQ brings us back to considering your odds.

In our view, unless there's only a 5 percent chance of rain, we strongly believe in bringing an umbrella with you on your journey through retirement. That is, *unless your RSQ is 95 percent or above*, we recommend an umbrella to protect you from fickle markets, the sequence of returns, unpredictable inflation storms, and uncompensated longevity risk—and the umbrella we recommend is *product allocation*. If you want to be protected in all kinds of weather, then allocate your investable assets (your nest egg) between different investment *products* to increase your RSQ.

So after you've calculated your RSQ, where do we go next? It depends on your RSQ. If your RSQ is already above 95, you are pretty much done. There is no need for you to use product allocation to increase the sustainability of your retirement income. You

Exhibit 16.1: The Seven Steps to Pensionize Your Nest Egg: Step 5

4 Calculate Your Retirement Sustainability Quotient

5 Assess Your Plan: Is it Sustainable?

6 Calculate Your Financial Legacy Value

have a pension gap, but your RSQ is sufficiently high that you don't need to take any further steps to secure your retirement income for life. You do, however, need to double-check your inflation and tax assumptions.

However, if your RSQ is something between 50 and 95, continue to our next step, which will show you how to use the power of product allocation to pensionize your nest egg.

And if your RSQ is less than 50, at this point we recommend that you go back to Step 1 and make some tough choices about your existing retirement plan—by choosing to spend less in retirement, rethinking the timing of your retirement decision, or saving more to support your retirement income goals. A financial economist would say that your desired lifestyle far exceeds your lifetime resources.

Now, you may think this advice is too generic and doesn't apply to your situation. We hope we've convinced you, through our discussion of the risks in retirement in Part I, that even the most risk-loving retiree should consider insuring against inflation, longevity, and sequence of returns risks. But whatever you do, we hope we've at least awoken you to the risks you face. The point of Step 5 is just to see where you are and what your next step will be. If you are continuing on through the Seven Steps, your next step is to answer the question, "What's it all about—me or the kids?"

Are you ready? Let's continue on to Step 6, considering your financial legacy.

Recap of Step 5

- ✓ The goal of Step 5 is to assess your RSQ and figure out your next step. Are you done, going forward to steps 6 and 7, or going back to Step 1?
- ✓ The result of your RSQ will give you the recommended next step.

17

Step 6: Calculate Your Financial Legacy Value

We are almost done! The last big conversation we need to have before you are set up to pensionize your nest egg is about the trade-off between your income in retirement (when you are alive) and your financial legacy (after you have passed on).

Now, we've gone over the theoretical aspects of this conversation several times already, in Part II. What you need to do now is figure out the value that you want to leave as a financial legacy. Whatever number it is, you need to identify this amount so you can assess your plans going forward.

To complete this step, you need to know if you'd be satisfied with (to use one extreme example) no assets left over at the end of life—or

Exhibit 17.1: The Seven Steps to Pensionize Your Nest Egg: Step 6

5 Assess Your Plan: Is It Sustainable?

6 Calculate Your Financial Legacy Value

7 Use Product Allocation to Pensionize™ Your Nest Egg

even living on borrowed money—or if you really need and expect to have $100,000, $250,000, or $500,000 left as a legacy. Now, we know that your total legacy may include lots of non-financial (in the sense of investable) assets that nonetheless have value, from grandmother's silverware to the family cottage. For this calculation, we are only taking into account your investable assets.

You don't need to worry about plotting any frontiers on a graph—you just need to know how much of your current assets you'd like to leave behind. The calculator at www.qwema.ca will help you with this issue, as it will calculate the FLV of your retirement income plan at the same time as it calculates your plan's RSQ.

The answer to this question will really help you evaluate your retirement income plans, including how much to pensionize. We've said already that the frontier is inevitable: you can't avoid it, and instead you should make sure you are comfortable with the place you end up. We will explore this conversation much more deeply in the next section, which includes a basic case study examining different plans that lead to different spots on the frontier.

Recap of Step 6

✓ The goal of Step 6 is to figure out what amount you'd like to leave as a financial legacy.

✓ Once you have that number in mind, you are ready to move on to the final step—using product allocation to pensionize your nest egg.

18

Step 7: Use Product Allocation to Pensionize the Right Fraction of Your Nest Egg

The very last step is to actually pensionize the right fraction of your nest egg by allocating your resources across the three available product silos.

So, how does this work? Working through this step requires you to bring together much of the thinking we've done so far, including determining your desired Financial Legacy Value. Now, there are many factors that will affect how you actually put product allocation into place and many choices and decisions you will need to make.

We'll consider one case study example in detail so you can see how product allocation might work in practice. Along the way, you'll learn how to use our calculator to estimate your own retirement sustainability score and the Financial Legacy Value of your personal retirement income plans. Keep in mind that this case study is simply intended to illustrate some concepts-any real-life situation will be much more complex than this example.

Exhibit 18.1: The Seven Steps to Pensionize Your Nest Egg: Step 7

6 Calculate Your Financial Legacy Value

7 Use Product Allocation to Pensionize™ Your Nest Egg

Case Study: Jack and Jill Go Up the Hill (to Fetch a Retirement Income Plan)

Let's take the case of Jack, age 69, and Jill, age 67. They are retired, but don't really have a retirement income plan. They have recently learned about the concepts of Retirement Sustainability Quotient and the Financial Legacy Value, and they'd like to know where they sit on the retirement income frontier. (The kids, in particular, want to know more about their mom and dad's expected FLV!)

We'll look at where Jack and Jill's current retirement plan puts them, at whether they have an RSQ score that works for them, and at steps they might take to improve their sustainability score. Is pensionizing part of their nest egg a wise choice for them?

Jack and Jill have amassed a nest egg worth $850,000 today. All of these assets are sitting inside RRSPs, which means all money from their nest egg will be taxable as income as it is withdrawn. (The calculations they will need to make would be a bit more complicated if they had a mix of taxable and tax-deferred assets, but the underlying idea is the same whether assets are taxable or not.)

In addition, they are going to go through the steps to pensionize their nest egg as if they have one portfolio. In reality, they have a mix of assets, some held by Jill and some by Jack. However, during their marriage they have never considered their assets separately, so they are going to take on this project—pensionizing their nest egg—as a single unit, consistent with how they've handled their finances so far in life.

Step 1: Identify Your Desired Retirement Income

After going through a budgeting exercise, the couple has decided they would like $65,000 annually (approximately) in consumable, real (inflation-adjusted) dollars. Note that this is the amount they would like after-tax—they'd like about $5,400 coming into their bank account every month, which they can spend as they please. Truthfully, they didn't spend a lot of time coming up with this number. They know they will review it more closely as they work through the Seven Steps, so they decided to start with this ballpark amount.

The first big step they need to take is converting their desired yearly after-tax spending to a pre-tax amount. This will allow them to figure out how much they need to withdraw from their savings each year to provide them with $65,000 to spend. Using a financial calculator and information from their tax returns, they figure their average total tax rate is about 35 percent. (And again, they are estimating a single average rate for both of them, not individual rates that they would apply to different fractions of their nest egg.)

This is a slightly conservative estimate, as they expect their actual tax rate in future years to be a little below 35 percent (so long as they keep making donations to charity and taking advantage of other tax credits and deductions). But they would rather be conservative in their estimates and have a little extra left over, than be overly optimistic and find themselves falling short of funds.

So, in order to determine how many pre-tax dollars they'll need to provide $65,000 after tax (with a 35 percent tax rate), they need to do a little bit of algebra. We went over this earlier, too. Here's the equation they need to solve:

$$\textit{Gross amount} = \textit{desired annual income} / (1 - \textit{tax rate})$$

Here are the specific values for Jack and Jill:

Gross amount = *$65,000 / (1 − 0.35)*

Solving this equation gives them the gross amount of $100,000: this is the amount they need to withdraw from their portfolio each year to get $65,000 in after-tax income. As we said earlier, you can use this simple equation, too, to find out your required pre-tax withdrawals to get your desired after-tax income.

Jack and Jill have now completed Step 1, and have estimated the amount of pre- and after-tax income they'd like in retirement.

Step 2: Estimate Your Existing Pensionized Income

Jack and Jill have a total of $17,000 in public pension income, from a mix of CPP and OAS. They will receive a portion of full CPP and some OAS based on their work history and residency in Canada. This income is fully taxable and they have no other pensionized income.

Jack and Jill have now completed Step 2: adding up their existing pensionized income.

Step 3: Determine Your Pension Income Gap

The next step is for the couple to estimate their yearly pension income gap—that is, the gap between the amount they want to spend and the amount of pension income they have coming in each year.

Now, just a moment ago we said that Jack and Jill estimate they will receive a total of $17,000 in *pre-tax* CPP income each year, and you'll remember that Jack and Jill have worked out that they need $100,000 of *pre-tax income* each year.

So, in order to take these pre-tax dollars into account in calculating their pension income gap, they subtract the pre-tax amount of CPP from the pre-tax withdrawals required from their portfolio.

This calculation gives them their *pension income gap*, which is $83,000 (or $100,000–$17,000). This is the amount of pre-tax income they must withdraw per year from their RRSPs (and later, their RRIFs) so that they get the after-tax $65,000 they desire.

Jack and Jill have now completed Step 3: they have calculated their pension income gap.

Step 4: Calculate Your Retirement Sustainability Quotient

The next question Jack and Jill need to consider is whether their plan (to withdraw $83,000 per year from their nest egg) is sustainable, that is, whether it has a sufficiently high Retirement Sustainability Quotient. Remember that we've said the RSQ is a little bit like a weather forecast, and you want to protect yourself against the chance of rain (running out of money) during your expected lifetime.

As we've said, Jack and Jill have a total of $850,000 in RRSPs, split between them. Because we are assuming one tax rate for both of them, it isn't important to sort out who owns the funds for this calculation. The overall asset allocation in their various RRSPs is roughly 60 percent in stocks and 40 percent in bonds. The real (or inflation-adjusted) rate of return they expect on their portfolio is 3.68 percent, which is also called the geometric mean return. (This rate of return reflects our expectations about the financial economy, and these expectations are "baked into" the calculator on the www.qwema.ca website.)

Now Jack and Jill have all the information they need to calculate the RSQ of their retirement plan. If they make no changes to their asset or product allocations, how *sustainable* is their plan to withdraw an inflation-adjusted, pre-tax income of $83,000 each year? And what's their Financial Legacy Value with this plan?

The couple used the calculator at www.qwema.ca to determine their RSQ and FLV values.

Exhibit 18.2: The QWeMA Group Retirement and Sustainability Calculator

www.qwema.ca

If you are interested in computing Legacy and Sustainability values for other cases, please go to the calculators section of www.qwema.ca

Here's what they discovered: if they don't pensionize any more of their wealth and simply continue with their current plan, they have an RSQ score of just under 42 percent and a Financial Legacy Value of just under $93,000. These values were calculated by multiplying the 100 percent certainty of their pensionized income by one minus the probability of ruin for the rest of their income stream (or $83,000).

(This explanation may be a little technical, but to calculate the probability that some event will *not* happen—in this case, the probability that they will not run out of money before they run out of life—we subtract from one the probability that it will. This rule for calculating probabilities is taken from the general field of probability theory, which is the branch of mathematics concerned with the analysis of random phenomena.)

Jack and Jill have now completed Step 4: they have calculated the sustainability and financial legacy of their current plans.

Step 5: Assess Your Plan: Is It Sustainable?

Is that good enough? Both Jack and Jill agree: they aren't willing to proceed any further in retirement with a plan that has a greater than 50 percent chance of failure. Instead, they want to explore alternatives to see if they can move their score higher without it decreasing their Financial Legacy Value.

Plan A: Spend Less

There are a couple of different ways they can approach this problem. The first one they want to explore is spending less in retirement. They pull out their financial statements again and take another look at their numbers. After some discussion, they conclude they would be willing to have a stable, inflation-adjusted retirement income of $45,000 after-tax. *Sustainability over the long term is more important to them than income in the near term*, they agree. (They know they can boost their yearly income by reducing the amount of tax they pay, and they are also expecting some OAS income each year to provide a little buffer.)

Now their pension income gap has moved from $83,000 to $52,000—due to the effects of tax. Although they have only reduced their after-tax spending by $20,000, the gap has closed by more than $20,000. (By reducing your after-tax spending by $1, you reduce the pre-tax withdrawals from your portfolio by more than $1, as pre-tax withdrawals need to include an additional amount for taxes payable, before the money ends up in your hands.)

Running the calculations again with the revised desired annual income figure, they can see that this choice immediately moves their RSQ to a much more acceptable 75 percent (versus 42 percent with yearly withdrawals of $65,000). It also more than doubles their expected financial legacy, moving it from $93,000 to $214,000.

However, Jack and Jill are not entirely comfortable with a retirement income plan that still only has a 75 percent chance of success.

Plan B: Pensionize a Fraction of Your Nest Egg by Buying an Annuity

After some more discussion, they decide that, in addition to reducing their spending level, they'll also consider purchasing an annuity. By spending $200,000 today to purchase an annuity, the total size of their nest egg does not change—*but more of it is pensionized.* Jack and Jill know (from reading this book) that increasing pensionization equals increasing sustainability. By how much does the sustainability of their retirement income plan change if they pensionize more of their nest egg, and what is the impact on their Financial Legacy Value?

Here's the answer they get from their calculations: by using $200,000 to purchase an annuity, they will get $12,800 more in annual, inflation-adjusted, pre-tax income each year, and the percentage of their nest egg that is pensionized jumps from 24 percent to 41 percent. (Note that their annuity income doesn't affect the amount of after-tax income they will receive each year; it just closes their pension income gap.) This in turn moves their sustainability score from 75 percent (mediocre) to 86 percent (much healthier), which is much more acceptable to them. *Now their pension income gap is $39,400*—less than half of what it was when they began.

Step 6: Calculate Your Financial Legacy Value

In Plan B, their financial legacy has moved from $93,000 (in their original plan) to $167,000. It isn't as high as it would be if they were to reduce spending but did not pensionize any (more) of their nest egg. However, as we have said, and this case study demonstrates, the Fundamental Theorem of Retirement Income Planning holds that if you want a higher RSQ, you must accept a lower FLV.

Now Jack and Jill have the beginnings of a workable plan. They can see, conceptually, the impact that pensionizing some fraction of their nest egg has on the sustainability and legacy of their retirement income plans. And importantly, they can see that it improves *both* the sustainability and legacy of their original starting point.

Exhibit 18.3 shows the changes in RSQ, FLV, the percentage of pensionized income, and the pension income gap for each of these three possible plans: their original starting point, Plan A (spend less), and Plan B (spend less and buy an annuity).

Step 7: Use Product Allocation to Pensionize Your Nest Egg

Now that they have the basic parameters of a plan set out, Jack and Jill can start to optimize their plan along the retirement income frontier. They can, for example, experiment with pensionizing more of their nest egg. They can also change the asset allocation in their RRSPs. In addition, Jack and Jill's paths will vary with their circumstances, needs and wants.

Jack and Jill may not like the idea of irreversibly pensionizing a fraction of their nest egg using a life annuity. This is where a GLWB may come in handy for them—because this hybrid product allows them to retain the funds in their nest egg while generating pensionized income from those funds. Now, to compute the RSQ for a nest egg allocation that includes products from all three silos is beyond the scope of this book. You will need to consult with a financial advisor to work through scenarios and plans that include GLWBs. However, it is important to note that this course of action will not

Exhibit 18.3: Jack and Jill's Pensionization Process

STARTING POINT		Pension Income Gap	% of Nest Egg Pensionized™	RSQ	FLV
Nest Egg (pre-tax)		$83,000	23.8%	41.6%	$92, 893
Plan A Reduce Spending	Reduce desired after-tax income				
Result	–$20,000	$52,231	23.8%	75.4%	$214,080
plus Plan B Pensionize™	Spend $200,000 on Life Annuity				
Result	+$12,798	$39,433	41.7%	85.4%	$167,094

increase your RSQ as much as a "true" annuity, but it will provide greater liquidity and a higher expected financial legacy.

Summary of Part III

We have now reached the end of Part III, and we've worked through one example of how a couple might pensionize their nest egg. We've reviewed each of the steps along the way to pensionization, and hope that we've set you up to start to work out your own plans. But more than that, we hope we've opened up some new ways to think about retirement income planning and provided some new strategies to consider as you move forward with this stage of life.

Final Thoughts

Most books on personal finance try to provide comprehensive advice on all aspects of wealth management and investment planning. Chock full of tips, suggestions, and ideas for helping you improve all the monetary aspects of your life, they aspire to become the encyclopedic go-to location for all things financial.

As you can probably tell, this is not that kind of book. In contrast to most other books about managing your money, we feel quite comfortable summarizing the main idea of this entire book in one simple sentence:

If you don't have a pension—and you probably don't—make sure to go out and buy one.

Everything we said in this book was our attempt to make the case for why this one idea is so important. Along the way, we defined the characteristics of a true pension and challenged you to confirm whether or not you have one. We provided some guidelines for how to determine whether your pension will truly protect your retirement, and we offered some suggestions about modern pension products that can help fill in your pension income gap.

Our motivation for writing this book came from the hundreds of discussions we've had on the topic of retirement income security. Over the years, when we asked people from all walks of life the very basic question: "Are you on track for a secure retirement?" we got two general types of answer. The first kind of response was a sheepish admission that, "No, I'm worried, and I should probably be contributing more to my RRSP." The second type of response was a more optimistic, "Yes, I will be okay; I am contributing the maximum to my RRSP."

We believe that both responses are incorrect and alarming. We have probably said this at least half a dozen times so far, and we will say it again one final time: a Registered Retirement Savings Plan, Tax Free Savings Account, permanent or whole life insurance policy, or any large sum of money in a mutual fund, segregated fund, or discount brokerage account is *not a pension*. It only has the potential to become a pension if you convert it into a pension.

A pension is a very specific contract between you and a pension provider. A true pension protects you against risks and guarantees a secure, predictable, inflation-adjusted lifetime income for you and your spouse. No ifs, ands, or buts allowed. Recall that we described the new risks that emerge when you enter retirement, including the Dragon of Decaying Dollars, the Spectre of Longevity Risk, and the Serpent of the Sequence of Returns. Pensionization—the process of generating your own pension income using the products available today—is the best shield we know of to protect you against these new risks.

Sure, if you want to wait for politicians and public policy experts to fix the Canadian pension system, then be our guest. And true, there is a group out there that is fully pensionized and doesn't need any more help at all, but they are in the minority. Instead, we believe you should take your retirement income security into your own hands and make sure you have some sort of predictable, longevity-insured income; that is, a true pension.

Currently in Canada, you can only purchase a personal pension from an insurance company. They are licensed to sell all sorts of pension-like products that protect against the major risks you will face during retirement and which we've described in this book. Perhaps in the future the Canadian *Bank Act* will be revised and you will be able to purchase a pension directly, in a bank branch, or maybe from the Finance Department in Ottawa. But for right now, we just want to ensure you understand the risks of not using pension products.

How much you pensionize, when you start the process of pensionization, and exactly what type of products you use is up to you (and perhaps your financial advisor). In fact, if you are new to money and finance or just don't enjoy this part of life very much, we strongly urge you to hire an expert and outsource the stress. Moreover, this book was never intended to provide all the answers. We wanted to give you a good place to start, not to tell you where you should end up. Instead of all the answers, our intention was to pose this simple question: *Do you have a pension, really?*

Finally, one of the nice things about writing a book with only one basic message is—it's certainly memorable!

Notes

Introduction

1. In the Introduction, we said that extensive studies have shown that people with pensionized income are happier than people without. To learn more, take a look at the studies by Panis (2003) and Bender (2004), referenced in the Bibliography.

Chapter 1

1. A modified and earlier version of this chapter was published as "What is a pension, exactly? (and why should you care?)" in the March 2010 issue of *Policy Options Politiques* on "Canadians and Their Pensions." This article is available from the website of the Institute for Research on Public Policy at www.irpp.org.
2. Exhibit 1.2 includes data on the entire Canadian labour force, including self-employed workers. Exhibit 1.3 does not include data on 2.7 million self-employed workers.
3. The chart in Exhibit 1.1 was developed with assistance from Melissa Martin, Producer of TVO's *The Agenda with Steve Paikin*. The authors are grateful for the assistance.
4. Permission to quote an excerpt from the *Globe and Mail* article entitled "Ottawa won't aid GM pension plan" was granted to the authors by CTVglobemedia publishing on May 28, 2010.
5. In Chapter 1 and throughout the book estimates of longevity probabilities were calculated using male, female, and unisex mortality data from Statistics

Canada's life tables for Canada, Catalogue no. 84-537-XIE. Annuity and pension payout rates were calculated using slightly more optimistic longevity assumptions, also known as the RP2000 mortality tables.

6. For estimates of indexed (inflation-adjusted) annuities, we have assumed annuity quotes are valued based on a long-term interest rate of 2 percent. For non-indexed annuities, we have assumed 4 percent is the annual valuation rate used to discount future cash flows. This is an assumption, but not that far from reality in mid-2010.
7. To read more about life-cycle thinking and the utility value of pensions, go to the classic work by Modigliani (1986) and recent book by Burns and Kotlikoff (2008), listed in the Bibliography.

Chapter 3

1. Exhibit 3.1: The Sally, David, and Robert scenarios were based on the assumption of 180 months of saving starting in May 1984 and calculated every 5 months until March 2010. We have assumed (for David and Robert only) mutual fund management expense ratios (MERs) of 2 percent.
   - For Sally, we used monthly Canadian T-Bill rates (calculated as annual rate/12).
   - For Robert, we tracked S&P/TSX composite total return and assumed deposits at month-end.
   - For David, we tracked S&P500 Total Monthly Return (in CAD$) using US total monthly return and adjusting each month's return using the interbank exchange rate. Again, we assumed deposits at month-end. Information about the percentage of actively-managed mutual funds which had 5-year returns in excess of index returns was taken from the Standard and Poor's index versus active funds scorecards for Canadian (June 2010) and U.S. funds (March 2010). Both reports are available at www.standardandpoors.com.
2. Data from 2008 about RRSP contributions, the total available RRSP room and the median contribution are drawn from Statistics Canada, CANSIM tables 111-0039 and 111-0040.

Chapter 4

1. All data about current and past inflation rates in Canada was sourced from the online inflation calculator available at the Bank of Canada website at www.bankofcanada.ca.

2. The data in Exhibit 4.1: *How a Dollar Decays over Time* is based on April CPI calculations for each year.
3. Data about changes in various components of the Consumer Price Index is drawn from Statistics Canada, principally *The Consumer Price Index – February 2010* (Catalogue no. 62-001-X) and CANSIM table 326-0020.
4. Research about the different spending patterns of senior households and whether the CPI is a good measure of price increases faced by individual households, including senior households, is available in the analytical article *Is Inflation Higher for Seniors? 1992 to 2004* from Statistics Canada, Catalogue no. 11-621-MWE2005027.

   We note as well an interesting idea from Malcolm Hamilton (received via private correspondence with the authors) on the topic of inflation protection in retirement. He has suggested that a useful product in retirement would be an annuity that increases at CPI-2% - to account for declining consumption in retirement, while providing a rising income if inflation exceeds 2%.

Chapter 6

1. You can read more about one example of the reaction of pensioners when asked to switch from DB to DC pension plans in the article by Milevsky and Promislow (2004), "Florida's Pension Election: From Defined Benefit to Defined Contribution and Back Again." See the Bibliography for the full reference.
2. To learn more about the protection available to policyholders for annuity payouts, go to the website www.assuris.ca.

Chapter 8

1. All data in the Exhibit 8.3: *GLWBS: Issuers, Features and Benefits* are drawn from prospectuses valid at the time of publication. Readers are cautioned that this information is subject to change without notice. The authors would also like to acknowledge Investor Economics, Inc. for information on the ranking of GLWB issuers in Canada.

Chapter 9

1. For Exhibit 9.2: *Nest Eggs, Pensionization, and Your RSQ*, we assumed a 60-year-old unisex retiree who received $2 of lifetime income for $33.3.

   We assumed that investable wealth at retirement was allocated to a diversified portfolio consisting of 60 percent stocks and 40 percent bonds. The stocks are expected to earn approximately 6 percent real after-inflation (and after management fees) returns, but with a variability of plus/minus 20 percent.

We also assumed that the inflation-adjusted yield on long-term bonds was approximately 2 percent, again, after all fees.

All of this implies that a diversified 60/40 portfolio of stocks and bonds should grow (using the geometric mean) by approximately 3.7 percent in real terms, with a variability of approximately 12 percent per year.

Finally, we assumed that the inflation-adjusted life annuity embedded within this example was priced off the 2 percent real yield, and assuming a (Canadian) mortality model that implies a 5 percent probability of survival to age 100 and an exponentially declining survival rate. We did not assume population mortality rates for annuity pricing and RSQ calculations.

Chapter 11

1. The information for Exhibit 11.3: *The Ongoing Costs to Pensionize* is drawn from Morningstar.ca; the study on mutual fund fees around the world by Khorana, et al. (2007), and the Morningstar study of Global Fund Investor Experience by Rekenthaler, et al. (2009). See the Bibliography for complete information on these sources. Note that we have focused on ongoing management fees only, and are not implying in any way, shape, or form that immediate annuities are costless or provided on a pro-bono basis by the insurance company.

Chapter 13

1. Information on the percentage of Canadians who have their OAS "clawed back" is taken from the website of Human Resources and Skills Development Canada at www.hrsdc.gc.ca.

Chapter 15

1. As throughout the book, the calculator noted in Chapter 15 is built on the following assumptions:
   - A Gompertz approximation to mortality
   - A risk-free rate of 2 percent
   - Equity returns of 6 percent and volatility of 20 percent.

   These factors are subject to change without notice. Any future changes to these assumptions will be noted on the calculator itself.

Bibliography

Bender, Keith A. "The Well-Being of Retirees: Evidence Using Subjective Data." Boston: Center for Retirement Research at Boston College, October 2004.

Bodie, Zvi and Michael J. Clowes. *Worry-Free Investing: A Safe Approach to Achieving Your Lifetime Financial Goals.* New Jersey: Financial Times Prentice Hall, Pearson Education Inc., 2003.

Burns, Scott and Laurence J. Kotlikoff. *Spend 'Til the End: Raising Your Living Standard in Today's Economy and When You Retire.* New York: Simon & Schuster, 2010.

Cohen, Bruce and Brian Fitzgerald. *The Pension Puzzle: Your Complete Guide to Government Benefits, RRSPs, and Employer Plans, 3rd ed.* Canada: John Wiley & Sons Canada, Ltd., 2007.

Khorana, Ajay, Henri Servaes, and Peter Tufano. "Mutual Funds Fees Around the World." HBS Finance Working Paper No. 901023, July 23, 2007.

Ibbotson, Roger G., Moshe A. Milevsky, Peng Chen, and Kevin X. Zhu. "Lifetime Financial Advice: Human Capital, Asset

Allocation, and Insurance." The Research Foundation of CFA Institute, 2007.

Milevsky, Moshe A. and S.D. Promislow. "Florida's Pension Election: From Defined Benefit to Defined Contribution and Back." *Journal of Risk and Insurance*, vol. 71, no. 3, 2004: 381–404.

Modigliani, Franco. "Life Cycle, Individual Thrift, and the Wealth of Nations." *American Economic Review*, American Economic Association, vol. 76, no. 3 June 1986: 297–313.

Panis, Constantijn W.A. "Annuities and Retirement Satisfaction." The RAND Corporation. Labor and Population Program, Working Paper Series 03–17. April 2003.

Reichenstein, William. "Calculating Asset Allocation." *The Journal of Wealth Management*, Fall 2000.

Rekenthaler, John, Michelle Swartzentruber, and Cindy Sin-Yi Tsai. "*Global Fund Investor Experience*." Morningstar Fund Research, May 2009.

Acknowledgements

The authors would like to acknowledge the able research assistance of Natalie Argiropoulos and the technical support of Kevin Lin and Faisal Habib, all current or former employees of The QWeMA Group. Thanks are also due to Warren Huska for illustration and graphics support and to Edna Diena Milevsky for her constructive contributions throughout the lifetime of this project.

Finally, the draft manuscript benefitted from careful reading and thoughtful comments from several outside readers. We are grateful for the ideas and input from Josef Frank, assistant vice president of of fixed products and retirement solutions with Manulife Investments; Malcolm Hamilton, Principal with Mercer Human Resource Consulting Limited; Lowell Aronoff, CEO of CANNEX Financial Exchanges Limited; Tina Di Vito, Director of the BMO Retirement Institute; and Jason Pereira of Woodgate Financial Partners/Bennet March/IPC Investment Corporation. Despite the wide array of readers who participated in shaping this manuscript, the authors alone retain responsibility for any errors and omissions.

About the Authors

Moshe A. Milevsky, Ph.D., is an author, researcher and professor at York University in Toronto, Canada.

Alexandra C. Macqueen is a Certified Financial Planner professional who works as a project manager at The QWeMA Group in Toronto, Canada.

Index

Page numbers in *italics* indicate a figure or chart.

A

accumulation-focused accounts, 62
accumulation phase, 44, 61
adverse selection (life annuity), 75
after-inflation terms, 160
after-tax funds (annuities), 71
after-tax income, 155–157, 177–178
age of death, 21–22
annual inflation rate, 50, *50*, 52
annual investment returns, cyclical, 39
annual management expense ratio, 130–131
annuities
  as gamble, 77–80
  as illiquid, 76
  and implied return, 80
  and inflation, 83–84
  and interest rates, 82–83
  and investment returns, 76
  joint, 71
  payouts, *73*
  payouts, and insurance, 85
  payouts, and smooth income stream, 106
  questions about, 62
  risks, 132
  in silo, 64
  term, 71
annuitize wealth, 62
arithmetic average earning rate, 38
asset allocation
  calculate, 163
  and case study, 179–180
  product, 61
  and risk, 88
  traditional, 87–88
asset instability, 46
assets, 163–164
Assuris, 85
average return (stock market), 39, *40*
average tax rate, 156–157

B

bank term deposit, 75
bear cycle, 44
bear market, 41, 44, 45, 165
benchmark rate, 83
biostatistics, 26
bond ladder, 90–91
bonds
  allocating, 62, 88
  and asset allocation, 87, 164
  behaviour, 164
  and retirement, 33–36
  in silo, 64, 89
borrowing, and longevity, 30
bridge players, 77–79
bucketing strategy, 45
budgeting, 138, 159
bull market, 41
buy-and-hold, 33, 34, *35*

C

cable TV, 56
calculating present value, 41
calculator
  free, 165
  ILY, 83
  online, 150
  for pension gap, 165, 166
  QWeMA, 167, *180*
Canada Pension Plan, 141, 146, 148
Canadian equity mutual funds, 36, 71
Canadian household spending, 138, *139*, 140
Canadian stock market, 34, 39
Canadian stocks, 62
CANNEX, 83
capital, drawing down, 106
capital accumulation plan, 14
car insurance, 84
case study, 176–183
cash, 18, 88
chance, 169
chance of survival, 78
children
  and assets, 120
  as awkward subject, 120, 170
  borrowing from, 30
  caring for parents, 19
  gifts to, 142
  and great-grandma's gamble, 77, 79
  and life annuity, 74
  and parents' retirement, 19
  and risk, 67
civil servants, 152
clerical workers, 54
clockwise investment returns, 40
collective saving and investment plan, 14
commodities, 88
commuting benefits, 151
commuting pension benefits, 152
compound rate of return, 33
Confederation Life, 85
constant earning rate, 38–39
constant returns, 41
constant spending level, 107
constant withdrawal rate, 106, 107
Consumer Price Index (CPI), 51, 54–55, 57, 83
consumption smoothing, 105
contractive value, 94, 95
contract value, 94, 96
conventional instruments, in silo, 88
conventional interest-bearing instruments, 75–76
conventional investment products, 87
corporate bond, 75–76
corporate pension plan, 15

cost of living
and DB pension, 151–152
and inflation, 52
and life annuity, 70
and pension gap, 159
and products, 57
cost of pension guarantee, 18
counter-clockwise returns, *42*, 42–43
CPI, 51, 54
CPI-E, 54, 56
CPI-W, 54
CPP
and average tax rate, 156
changes to, 149
estimating, 149
and income gap, 157
and inflation, 148
for injured workers, 148
and low-income seniors, 148
as national program, 146
proposals, 9
as true pension, 19
yearly statements, 150
credit rating, 85
creditworthiness, 85
current after-tax income, 141
current expenses, 142
cyclical returns, 41

D

dating services, 131
David, 34–36, 46, 71, 72
day-to-day spending, 138
defind benefit pension plan (DB)
benefits, 150–152
commuted value, and tax, 152
commuting benefits, 151
coverage, decline in, 14
and DC, compared, 19–20
and DC pension plan, 77
and default, 152
and defaulting, 16
and employers, 10
estimating income, 150–152
leaving, 152
and longevity risk, 31
members, *12*, 13, *13*
non-inflation-adjusted, 160
and private sector workers, 13
and public sector workers, 13
and risk of default, 152
and RSQ, 111
in silo, 63, 64, 88
defined contribution pension plan (DC)
and annuities, 71
coverage, 14
and DB, compared, *12*, 19–20
described, 10–12
as money purchase plan, 10
and RSQ, 111
in silo, 88
death benefit, 123, 124
default, pension plan, 152
default retirement age, 153
deferred annuity, 73
deferred income annuity, 70
defined profit sharing plan, 71
delaying withdrawals, GLWB, 95–96, *96*
Department of Labor (U.S.), 54
desired after-tax income, 157
desired income, 142
desired retirement income, 137–143, 157
de Tonti, Lorenzo, 80
disability insurance, 84
diversification, 87, 88
dividing assets, 163–164
dividing funds, 163–164
dollar-cost averaging (DCA), 37

downside protection, 33
Dragon of Decaying Dollars, xi, 50, 84
drawing down wealth, 109
drop-out, QPP, CPP, 148

E

employed, defined, 11–12
equities, 35
equity, 33
equity-based strategies, 72
equity investing, 35, 88
equity markets, 89
equity mutual funds, 36
escalating income annuity, 84
estimating required income, 138
exchange-traded funds (ETFs), 35, 64, 88, 89, 164
existing pension income, 145–154
expenses, estimating, 138
extended health care, 55

F

fictional savers, 34–36, 71, 72
financial advisors, 21, 131
financial crisis, 35
financial economics, 101–118
financial economics glasses, 106, 107
financial legacy, calculation, 173–174
Financial Legacy Value (FLV). *See* FLV
financially engineered products, 63
financial planners, 21
financial planning, 101–118
financial planning approach, 102
financial resources, and lifespan, 29–30
fixed-income instrument, and mortality credits, 83
fixed withdrawals, 38
floods, 107
FLV, 122–129
calculating, 175, 182–184
and pensionization, *128*
and retirement income, 131
and spending rate, *128*
formal pension plan, 8
Fundamental Theorem of Retirement Income Planning (Fundamental TRIP), 126, 127, 182
future pensions, 8

G

gains, DC pension, 11
gasoline, 56
General Motors of Canada, 7
generic retiree, 114
geometric average inflation rate, 51
Gertrude, 1–4
GIC, 64, 75–76, 91
GIS
and claw-back, 150
and CPP, 149
estimating, 150
and income, 149
as public program, 146
and RSQ, 167
and tax, 148
as true pension, 19
glasses, 102–103, 106, 120
Globe and Mail, 7, 21
GLWB
features, *98–99*, 100
fees, 97
history, 93
as income account, 65
and life annuity, 65
and life expectancy, 97
and mutual fund, 65
pendulum, 67
Protected Value, 94, 97

reset, 95, *95*, 96
sellers, 97, *98–99*, 100
and stock market, 65
GM pension plan, 7
government
employees, and pensions, 8
entity as counterparty to pension, 15
guarantee, pension plans, 13
Government of Canada, 19
government-sponsored programs, 63
Great-Grandma's Gamble, 77–80, *78*, 85
great money illusion, 50
Grim Reaper coin toss, 25
Gross Domestic Product (GDP), 111
Gross National Product (GNP), 111
ground-up estimate, 138, 141–142
group RRSP, 14
growth
potential, 66
rate, 33
stocks, 62
guarantee, and pension, 15
guaranteed income in retirement, 11, *12*, 31, 77
Guaranteed Income Supplement. *See* GIS
guaranteed lifetime income, 64
guaranteed lifetime withdrawal benefit products. *See* GLWBs
guaranteed monthly income for life, 64
guaranteed withdrawal base, 94, 96, 97

H

Harry, 3
health care, 56
home insurance, 84
household expenses, 138–140
household spending, Canada, 138
human capital, 103–104, 114
human longevity, 16
hybrid cars, 63
hybrid products, 88, 89, 90

I

ILY calculator, 83
immediate annuity, 70, 73, *73*
implied longevity yield (ILY), 83
income annuity products, 63, 130–131
income credit, GLWB, 95, 96
income for life, 93
income replacement rate, 20, 138
income stability, 45
income stream, 20, 93–94, 97
income tax, 140, 156
indexed annuities, 57
indexed life annuity, 17, 31, 83
index weight, CPI, 54
individual annuities, 71
individual probability, 28
infant mortality rate, 111
inflation, 49–57
affects on the elderly, 54
annual percentage rate, *53*
and annuities, 83–84
and cable, satellite TV, 56
and consumption, 160
and cost of living, 52
and DB pension, 151–152
and decay process, 51
and desired income, 142
and earning, 52
effects of, 53
and extended health care, 55
and gasoline, 56
index, 54
and investing, 56–57
low general rate, 51
and medical care, 55
and medication, 55

inflation (*Continued*)
and nursing homes, 55
and pension gap, 159
as personal, 56
and personal care, 56
and private transportation, 56
protection, 160
protection, and life annuity, 70
protection, repurchasing, 152
and public pension income, 160
and purchasing power, 49, 52
and retirement, 64
as retirement risk, 65
and spending habits, 54–55, 56
statistics, 51
and thinking, 56–57
and travel services, 56
inflation-adjusted apples, 160
injured workers, 148
insurance
actuaries, 25
company, and bankruptcy, 85
company as counterparty to pension, 15
event, 84
market, life annuity, 75
payoff, 69
and personal pension, 17
premiums, pension contributions as, 68–69
products, 75–76
and retirement risk, 67–71
and spouse, 69
interest rate
and annuities, 82–83
and cost of pension guarantee, 18
and cycles, 44
and life annuity, 75
underlying, 83
investable wealth, 15
investment
asset allocation portfolio, 37
fees, 36, 131
and fluctuation, 39
indexed to inflation, 57
and inflation, 57
and life annuity, 77
and next generation, 119–126
and real terms, 159
returns, 44
returns, in after-inflation terms, 160
issuers, GLWB, 97, *98–99*, 100

J

Jack, 176–183
Jill, 176–183
Joe Canuk, 127–129, 130
joint annuities, 71
joint-life annuities, 83
joint probability, 28

K

known returns, 38

L

labour force, 11–12, 14, *14*
Lamoureux, Claude, 8
leaving DB pension plan, 152
legacy, 119–126, 124–125, 173–174
life annuity, 67–71
age of purchase, 73
and bank term deposit, 75
and children, 74
cost of income, *74*, 75
and deferred payments, 73
as gamble, 77–80
and GIC, 75–76

and GLWB, 65
as insurance, 84–86
and investments, 77
and longevity risk, 77
and market risk, 77
monthly income, 72
prices, 75
reasons for, 72–75
and spouse, 74
when to buy, 72–73
life-cycle economics, 103, 105–106, 142
life-cycle model of consumption, 18, 20, 77, 106, 108
life expectancy, 76, 97, 108, 111
life insurance
and children, 124
and death benefit, 122
described, 70
eliminating, 140
and FLV, 123
as holding, 121
and seg fund, 94
selecting, 68
lifespan, 29–30, 110
lifetime consumption, 105
lifetime income, 10, 18, 79, 150
lifetime payout income annuity, 63
lifetime ruin probability, 16
limited withdrawals, GLWB, 93–94
longevity
and couples, 27–28
insurance, 66, 68–69, 79, 152
and life annuity, 75
predicting, 27
probabilities, 28
as retirement risk, 65
and women, 27
longevity numbers
average, 23–24
beyond 65, 22
and the stock market, 25, 26
longevity risk, 25–27
and allocation, 63
and DB pension, 31
insuring against, 29–30
and life annuity, 77
and ruin, 68
and SWP, 37
tolerance, 108
uncertainty, 30–31
longevity risk coin toss, 30
longevity tables, 111
loss of purchasing power, 49
lower income earnings, 148
low-income seniors, 148
lump sum cost, 73, 73–74
lump sum nest egg, 36

M

management fees, 130–131
margin of decay, 56
market
conditions, and retirement, 64
conditions and silo, 64
as retirement risk, 65
risk and life annuity, 77
markets, 37
maximum retirement payment, 150
medical care, 55
medications, 55
Members of Parliament, 8
meteors, 107
model, life-cycle, 18, 20
money purchase plan, 10
monthly income for life, 74
mortality-adjusted rates of return, 83
mortality credits, 70, 73, 75, 78, 79–80, 83, 109

mortgage, as expense, 140
mutual funds
and asset allocation, 164
and equities, 35
and fees, 36
and GLWB, 65
portfolio, 89
and retirement, 33
and risk, 87
as silo, 62
in silo, 64, 88

N

naked investments, 89
National Post, 8, 21
national public retirement income programs, 146
negative pension income gap, 157
negative return, 40
negative sequence of returns, 45, 165
noise, 44
non-pensionized assets, 129
non-pensionized wealth, 129
non-registered accounts, 64
normal retirement age, 152–153
Nortel Networks, 7, 16
nursing homes, 55

O

OAS
and claw-back, 147, 149, 150
estimating, 150
goal, 147
and guarantees, 19
plan, *146*
as public pension, 146
and replacement, 141
requirements, 147
tiered, 147
obituaries, 21, 26, 27
odds, 169
Old Age Security. *See* OAC
online retirement income calculator, 150
Ontario Teachers' Pension Plan, 8
Ottawa Citizen, 7

P

payout annuity, 84
payout periods, 70
pension. *See also* DB, DC, Q/CPP, OAS, GIS
annuities, and interest rates, 109–110
annuities, example, 116–117
annuities in silo, 88
and bankruptcy, 16–17
benefits, commuting, 152
as binding contract, 15
and bond, 69
contributions, as insurance premiums, 68–69
cost of, 17
coverage, decline, 14
coverage and labour force, 14
crisis, 7–9, 14
debate, 46
as describing DB and DC plans, 14
experts, 25
and guarantee, 15
income, estimating, 145–154, 178–179
income and spending, 109–110
income as buffer, 108–110
income sources, 145
and life-cycle model, 108
perceived usefulness of, 18
as product class, 15
what it is not, 15
pension gap
and annuity, 181–182
calculator, 165–167

and cost of living, 159
determining, 155–161
estimating, 178–179
filling, 164–168
and inflation, 159
and product allocation, 62
and savings, 163
and spending less, 181
and taxes, 155–157
pension income gap, 62
pension-like downside protection, 89
pension plan. *See also* DB, DC, Q/CPP, OAS, GIS
contributions, 10
decline in, 20
defined benefit vs defined contribution, *11*
and guarantees, 20
history of, 19
as household expense, 140
members, type of employment, 13
payout, 10
and public sector, 10
survivor, 10
pension retirement income, 157
pension survival probabilities, 108
personal balance sheet, 103–104
personal care, 56
personal inflation rate, 52, 54
personal pension
age of purchase, 80–82
buying, 69–71
as insurance, 84–86
reluctance, 37
phantom income credits, 96, 97
planned spending, 107
pooled funds, 164
population health, 75
population trends, 26
portfolio
diversified, and inflation, 57
longevity, 37–45
ruin, *38, 41, 43*
and sequence of returns, 37–45
positive pension income gap, 157
positive return, 40
predicting investment return, 37–39
preferred shares, 91
pre-pensionize, 146, 149
pre-retirement income, 141
present value, 41
pre-tax benefits, 150
pre-tax CPP income, 157
pre-tax dollars, 177–178
pre-tax income, 157
pre-tax withdrawals, 157
price fluctuation, 44
pricing model, 74
private sector pension plans, 14, 145
private sector workers, 13
private transportation, 56
probability distribution, 26, *26*, 27–28
probability of ruin, 180
probability of survival, 106
product allocation
defined, 62
and economic cycles, 62
as new basket, 61
and pension, 175–184, 183
questions, 62
risk and return characteristics, 62
product silos. *See* silos
profit-sharing plan, 14
provincial retirement income supplements, 146
public pension programs, 145, *146*
public pensions, 145–150
public sector, 10

public sector workers, 13
purchasing power, 49, 52

Q

Q/CPP
described, 146
and inflation, 148
and pre-retirement, 141
as true pension, 19
and yearly statement, 150
Q/CPP plans
income, *146*
timing, 152–153
QWeMA calculator, 165, 180
QWeMA Group, 22

R

reading glasses, *102*, 102–103, 106, 120
real products (inflation), 57
real terms, 56, 159
registered pension plan (RPP), 8, 9
representative consumer, 55
retirement
and desired after-tax income, 155–157
as household expense, 140
risks, 61
spending, 108
sustainability, 119–126
timing, 152–153
retirement accounts, 163
retirement age, 151
retirement income
calculator, 150
desired, 137–143
frontier, *122*
inflation projections, 56
and pension, 108–110
products, 63
prospects, 16
safety of, 8
silos, 64–66
streams, 16
system, 8
tiered, 147
yearly, 137–143
retirement income plan
creating, 37
and financial economics, 101–118
and financial planning, 101–118
fundamental theorem, 126
and RSQ, 110–116
structured, 87
retirement income planning, 33–36, 63
retirement longevity numbers, 22–25, *24*
retirement payment, 150
retirement risk, 65, 67, 88
retirement risk zone, 45
Retirement Sustainability Quotient. *See* RSQ
retirement sustainability score, 175
retirement wealth, forecasting, 110
rider, GLWB, 93, 97
rider, life annuity, 70
risk-averse retirees, 108
risk of default, 152
risk shifting, 19
risk tolerance, 108
risk-tolerant retirees, 108
Robert, 34–36, 46, 71, 72
Roman soldiers, 70
RPP (registered pension plan), 9
RRIF, 21, 64, 91, 165
RRSP
contribution room, 46
as household expense, 140
and income tax, 156
and individual annuities, 71

and living in retirement, 30
and RSQ, 111
in silo, 64
in SWP, 91
as tax-deferred account, 157
vs pension income, 110
RSQ, 110–116, 124–129
calculating, 165–167
and case study, 179–189
and current assets, 133
for generic retiree, *114*
number, 166–167
and pensionization, *128*
and product allocation, 169–170
and retirement income, 131
and spending rate, *128*
and time, 132
values, 117–118
RSQ calculator, 165–167
ruin age, 43
ruin probability, 112

S

safe withdrawal rate, 106
Sally, 34–36, 46, 71, 72
Saskatoon Star Phoenix, 7
satellite TV, 56
savings
plan, and RSQ, 111
and RSQ, 163
strategies, *36*, 105
segregated fund, 94
self-purchased pension, 72
sequence of returns, 37, 45, 65
sequence-of-returns-protected investments, 63
Serpent of the Sequence of Returns, xii
Service Canada, 150
seven steps, *138*
shares, in silo, 64
shelter, 140
silos, 62–66
allocation, 88
and annuities, 71
and GLWB, 93–95
and insurance, 117
and RSQ, 183
and SWP, 89–91
single-employer defined benefit pension plan, 8
solvency, 85
Spectre of Longevity Risk, xii
spending
Canadian households, 138–140, *139*
and ground-up estimate, 142
habits, 54–55, 56
levels, and total wealth, 113
plans, 127–129
in retirement, 108–110
and risk tolerance, 108
spending rate, 127
standard deviation, 23
standard of living, 30, 105, 106
Statistics Canada, 9, 26, 51, 54, 78, 81, 151
step up benefit, 95, 96
stock accounts, 62
stock and bond markets, 11
stock market
and GLWB, 65
and triangles, 44
vs lifetime annuity, 79
stocks
and allocation, 88
and asset allocation, 164
behaviour, 164
and retirement, 33–36
as risky, 87
in silo, 64, 89

survival probabilities, 107, 108
survival probability curve, 28–29
survivor pension, 10
sustainability/legacy frontier, 127–128
sustainability score, 128–129
synthetic income stream, 90
systematic withdrawal plan (SWP), 88–91

T

target replacement rate, 141
tax
    effect on income gap, 155–157
    and individual annuities, 71
    as portion of income, 156
    rate, estimating average, 156
Tax-Free Savings Account, 30, 64, 140, 165, 183
tax-sheltered accounts, 156
tax-sheltered savings, 9
T-Bills, 34, 37, 71, 72
temperature scales, 125
term annuities, 71
TFSA, 30, 64, 140, 165, 183
threshold rate, 83
today dollars, 160
tontine contract, 79–81, 82
top-down estimate, 138, 140, 141
Toronto Star, 21
traditional investment accounts, 87–91
transportation, 140
travel services, 56
true pension, defined, 20
TSX-based energy fund, 79
TSX Composite Index, 39

U

umbrella, 169
uncertainty, 30–31
underlying interest rate, 83
underlying investments, GLWB, 93
unexpected expenses, 142
United Airlines, 16
universal pensions, 9
urban wage earners, 54
U.S. equity mutual funds, 36, 71
U.S. stock market, 34
U.S. stocks, 62
utility value, 18

V

value stocks, 62
volume fluctuation, 44
von Bismark, Otto, 19

W

Wealth-to-Needs ratio (WtN), 15, 113–118, 132
wiggle room, 142
willingness to pay, 18
withdrawing resources, 104–107, 156–157
work paycheques, 9
workplace defined benefit pension, 145
workplace pension plan, *12*, 145

Y

yearly income, 137–143
years spent in retirement, 22–24, *23*
yield curve, 75